A Fortune
in
Free Real Estate

Featuring

The Equity Holding Land Trust™

Real Wealth Without Cash,
Credit or Management Costs

Bill J. Gatten, M.A. and Jan Caldwell, Esq.

A Fortune in Free Real Estate

ISBN: 0-9663302-2-6
Printed in the United States of America

IMPORTANT NOTICE

THIS BOOK CONTAINS REFERENCES TO VARIOUS INCOME TAX AND LEGAL ISSUES, WHICH INFORMATION IS NOT TO BE RELIED UPON WITH REGARD TO ANY SPECIFIC JURISDICTION, INSTANCE OR WITH RESPECT TO ANY PARTICULAR TRANSACTION OR BUSINESS OBJECTIVE. EACH NORTH AMERICAN REALTY SERVICES, INC. NEHTRUST™ TRANSACTION POSES A DISTINCTIVE SET OF CIRCUMSTANCES AND VARIABLE DATA, REQUIRING SEPARATE AND INDEPENDENT CONSIDERATION BY ONE'S OWN LEGAL AND FINANCIAL ADVISORS.

ALTHOUGH THE NORTH AMERICAN REALTY SERVICES, INC. NEHTRUST™ PROGRAM IS FULLY ENDORSED BY ITS OWN IN-HOUSE AND RETAINED OUTSIDE LEGAL COUNSEL AND ACCOUNTING ADVISORS, NORTH AMERICAN REALTY SERVICES, INC. IS NOT AN ACCOUNTANCY, LAW FIRM OR REAL ESTATE AGENCY, AND THEREFORE ADVISES ALL READERS TO EMPLOY THE SERVICES OF APPROPRIATE LICENSED PROFESSIONALS IN ALL RELATED MATTERS.

THIS BOOK IS EXPRESSLY NOT INTENDED TO IMPLY ANY ASSURANCES WITH RESPECT TO THE NATIONAL OR LOCAL ECONOMY, REAL ESTATE APPRECIATION, PROFIT POTENTIAL, OR THE ELIMINATION OF THE ORDINARY RISKS OF REAL ESTATE INVESTING AND/OR OWNERSHIP.

i

ABOUT THE AUTHORS

Bill J. Gatten, B.A., M.A., is an acclaimed author, lecturer, sales trainer, entrepreneur and Certified Seminar Leader. With degrees from the University of California and Cuesta College, San Luis Obispo, California, his richly varied background includes extensive experience in sales, sales training, banking, bank ownership, mortgage banking, capital equipment financing and real estate sales and investment.

Mr. Gatten is the founder of North American Realty Services, Inc. and the originator of the very unique and versatile land trust transfer methods described in this publication.

Anyone having worked with Bill Gatten, in any capacity, on real estate acquisitions and investments (buyers, sellers, Realtors®, mortgage bankers, mortgage brokers, income property owners, attorneys, accountants and real estate speculators) will readily affirm that, even beyond his vast knowledge and expertise, his contagious enthusiasm for the beneficial features of the NARS Equity Holding Trust™ concept is steadfast, and always intensely enriching.

Jan Caldwell, B.A., M.A., J.D. is a corporate and general business attorney. Raised in Illinois, she is a graduate of Kansas State University, Northwestern University and Loyola Law School, Los Angeles, California. She has been a member of the Maryland bar since 1987.

After twelve years in the Washington D.C. area working in government relations for a national trade association and in private practice as an attorney representing small and emerging businesses, Jan moved to California to be nearer her family. She is now employed as the Business Manager and In-House Legal Counsel for North American Realty Services, Inc.

ABOUT
NORTH AMERICAN
REALTY SERVICES, INC.

Founded by Bill J. Gatten in 1984 as "Resource Management Services," a sole proprietorship for the personal acquisition of real estate, the original company became a partnership between Mr. Gatten and Ms. Gail Akalp, later Mrs. Gatten, in 1989. Due to a decision to make its methods and services available to the real estate community in 1990, the company was subsequently re-formed and named "Cal-Equity Real Estate Consultants." Then in 1998, having gained national recognition and scope, the company underwent still another revamping and name change and incorporated as *North American Realty Services Inc.* (NARS). In order to spend more time teaching, mentoring and acquiring real estate, Mr. Gatten has recently asked Mrs. Gatten to serve as corporate president and CEO.

"NARS" is engaged in the business of professional consulting in residential and commercial real estate investing, sales, and sales training. Specializing in the NARS Equity Holding Land Trust™ Transfer System (the NEHTrust™), the company is known nationwide and is gaining acclaim within the real estate and real estate investment communities across the country.

Since making its programs available to the real estate community in 1990, NARS has emerged as singularly the most successful company of its type in the industry today. Having attracted many thousands of satisfied clients throughout the country via its seminar and workshop services, its programs and systems are considered to be among the safest and best available.

Aside from acquiring real estate for their own portfolio, the Gattens are heavily involved with their seminar and workshop services and NARS' Professional Realtor/Investor Network ,*"The NARS Network."* "The Network" is comprised of thousands of participating investors and Realtors® across the U.S. who receive regular training, coaching and mentoring in all aspects of the real estate business, as well as unlimited and ready sources of cash and sweat-equity partners for real estate investments.

NEHTrust™ transactions facilitated by NARS include, along with full Department of Real Estate (DRE) compliance in all states: documentation preparation; legal review and endorsement; payment collections and disbursement, trusteeships, personal buyer/seller client consultation; one-on-one consulting and training assistance; trust setup and collections from inception to termination. North American Realty Services, Inc. accepts full responsibility for preparation, construction, interpretation, and enforceability of the NARS Equity Holding Trust™ concept. It is important to note that—to date—never has a client, affiliate, broker or Certified Network Realtor ever been implicated in any manner in legal action or claim resulting from any aspect of the NARS NEHTrust™ documentation. Neither has there been a failure in, or unresolved impediment to, any eviction or trust termination process relative to default or nonperformance by any NEHTrust™ participant.

Contents

Forms

Formula for Bliss
H = R/D
Happiness (H) is the balance between Reward (R) and Desire (D)

When the *Reward* and *Desire* components of the above formula are unequal, *Happiness* is diminished in direct proportion to that inequality.

There is great joy in seeking the *Necessary* (needing) and knowing that when the goal is reached, the happiness derived will be at its zenith. On the other hand, *Wanting* without seeking (Hoping) can only bring unhappiness in the process, and a dismal dependence upon the most capricious and unreliable of all forces...*Luck.*

True *Happiness* will only be achieved by: 1) replacing hope with action (*Hope and Luck are the children of Helplessness*); 2) determining to obtain, regardless of the price, all of that which is truly needed; and 3) by giving to others everything attained that is in excess of what is essential.

In so much as the Universe abhors regression and vacuity, anything of value given without expectation, will invariably be replaced by something of greater worth: be it gratitude, adoration, love, money, more of what was given...or the greatest reward known to mankind... perfect contentment (*Bliss*).

Bill J. Gatten

A Fortune in Free Real Estate

ONE

THE NARS EQUITY HOLDING TRUST

Before proceeding with your reading of this book, ask yourself the following very important questions and keep them in mind as you proceed from page to page:

As a would-be real estate investor, would I accept a "free" house if offered, and if my only obligation would be assuring promptness of payments (while someone else makes them) and seeing to proper maintenance (while someone else does the work)?

As an investor or homeowner, should I insist on having my name on a property's deed (title) if without it I still had 100% of all the benefits of ownership, control, income tax write-off, and all profits produced by it...not to mention freedom from any party's lawsuits, creditor judgments or IRS tax liens attaching to my property?

Would a seller be better off selling a burdensome property at a loss and destroying his/her credit through foreclosure or lender compromise? Or...might that person fare better by having someone (me or someone I know) take over the mortgage and the care of the property, thus avoiding the prospect of further cash-drain and misery (i.e., the discomfort of having to hold and deal with an unwanted property)?

Might a seller be better off waiting a while to receive his hard-earned equity (or part of it) in cash, if it meant avoiding the standard costs of sale, price reduction and loss of large portions of what is supposed to have been "profit"?

Would a homebuyer with minimal cash and credit consider living in and making the payment on a nice home...perhaps even sharing the future profit potential with me, if I could provide them with 100% financing without bank qualifying or a standard down payment?

Would a landlord be better off if he/she could increase rental income and eliminate management, maintenance, and vacancies by selling all or portions of the property's profit centers to the tenant (equity, mortgage principal reduction, tax write-off, appreciation, etc.)?

The *NARS Equity Holding Trust™* (NEHTrust™ answers all of these questions and provides a unique and versatile means of safely and effectively acquiring, selling or investing in the benefits of *real property* ownership (real estate), without the necessity of new financing or standard down payment and credit requirements.

The combination of documents comprising the NEHTrust™ allows an owner (a would-be "seller") of real estate to place his/her property into a special revocable trust,[1] and sell all or a portion of the trust's beneficial interest to another party (i.e., the "buyer"), rather than effecting a transfer of the property's title itself. This means quick, safe, legitimate real estate acquisition without bank loans, down payments, credit applications or drawn-out escrow and approval processes.

Upon a person's receiving all or a portion of the *beneficial interest* in such a trust, he/she can henceforth be afforded virtually all of the same *income tax deduction, use, occupancy, possessory interest* and/or *profit-potential,* as would be any owner of real estate...but with far more asset protection and privacy of ownership.

2

Due to the fact that an assignment of beneficial interest in such a trust is, in effect, an assignment of an interest in *personal property*, rather than in *real property* (real estate), all the benefits of home ownership can be fully conveyed to another without jeopardy to the property or its title[2] or to the beneficiaries of the trust in which trust the title is vested with the selected trustee. Interestingly, in the process, even in view of the "payment takeover" by another, there is no open contravention of a mortgage lender's wishes relative to disposition of the property without a loan-payoff or formal assumption (re. the *"due-on-sale clause"* that is written into virtually all mortgage loans).[3]

As a matter-of-fact, the benefits for the "buyer" in a NEHTrust™ transfer are virtually identical to those in *any* real estate purchase; but far more protective and private. There is no necessity for any more credit qualification or down payment than the "seller" of the beneficiary interest might require (if any).[4]

By this simple (though safely documented) process, virtually any seller willing to keep the existing mortgage loan in place for a while, and willing to leave some or all of any equity in tact for the same period of time, can safely and effectively allow someone else to assume the responsibility for payments, taxes and insurance along with all income tax benefits. In so doing one is obviously relieved of the burdens of such obligations. In the NEHTrust™, the costs of property tax, insurance premiums and all upkeep and repair become the sole responsibility of the co-beneficiary.

The NEHTrust™ is truly a welcome reprieve for any overburdened seller who might be having a difficult time facing: impending foreclosure, bankruptcy, creditor litigation, divorce proceedings, IRS tax liens, probate issues, or who may be considering petitioning for an *offer and compromise* (short-sale) with the lender (the income tax credit damage ramification of which can be onerous).

Through the use of the NEHTrust™, one needn't face these issues with the threat of losing equity or enduring further credit damage. When used in lieu of foreclosure or short-sale, resultant credit damage and (fully taxable) "debt-relief,"[5] can be avoided. No longer does the overburdened homeowner need to walk away empty-handed from a troublesome, but otherwise valuable property. And no longer does an anxious seller need to resort to legally volatile "creative financing" schemes in order to escape an unwanted property.

If one were to be considering letting (renting or leasing) a property, as a solution to being unable to sell or obtain the right price, the NEHTrust™ will more than likely result in the superior and preferred means for eliminating concerns about negative equity, negative cash-flow, costly vacancies and maintenance and management expenses. A NEHTrust™ buyer, unable to qualify for the property otherwise, will gladly accept those responsibilities, in exchange for income tax benefits, all or a part of the appreciation potential and the myriad other benefits of homeownership.

Before we explore the NEHTrust™ in more detail, let us first review some of the many benefits and features that the overall structure provides buyers, sellers, real estate professionals and entrepreneurs alike.

Benefits for the Buyer

Compared with more common (and more precarious) forms of seller-assisted real estate financing (lease options, wraps, land contracts, equity shares, etc.), the NEHTrust™ provides the objectives of each of these

4

devices while allowing for all the same benefits of property ownership that acquisition by means of a new mortgage might, but with far less effort and more asset protection and:

1. Easiest credit qualification and payment arrangements (e.g., the buyer is qualified solely by the property owner on his/her own terms).[6]

2. Low, minimal or maybe even NO down payment. The NEHTrust™ buyer is often required to pay only closing costs, which may include just the escrow fee, miscellaneous trustee acceptance and setup fees and perhaps all or a portion of a Realtor's® commission—if a commission is involved.

3. Tax benefits. Though not on title, the trust beneficiary who is making payments, living in and managing the property is entitled to all income tax deductions for *mortgage interest* and *property taxes. See IRC §163(h)4(D).*

4. Equity buildup from the loan's principal reduction as the mortgage balance is reduced with each successive payment *(the older the loan at the start of the transaction, the more the loan is reduced by each successive payment).*

5. Potential for appreciation and profit.

6. Protection (shielding) of the property from creditor judgment, tax lien, lawsuit, bankruptcy, probate and/or legal claims in marital dispute by an [ex]spouse of either party (resident or nonresident beneficiary).

7. Pride-of-ownership. The *American Dream* and a slice of the proverbial *Apple Pie,* without all the rules and constraints of conventional real estate acquisition and mortgage financing requirements.

8. Ownership needn't impact a credit application or one's balance sheet. If shown anywhere, all that would appear (in a financial statement or credit application) is an interest in a real estate trust, not ownership of real estate. This means that debt and expenses relative to the property would not detract from one's net income.

9. Protection from illicit acts of the "other party/ies" (e.g., a seller's neglect in paying bills; non-responsiveness to local ordinances; imperiling the property's title by improper, illegal or neglectful acts).

10. No longer does one need to scrimp and save "forever" to begin enjoying the pride, freedom and benefits of homeownership.

Benefits for the Seller

When compared with virtually any "nontraditional" financing program, the NEHTrust™ affords maximum security for any seller contemplating OWC seller-financing (OWC = "Owner Will Carry") the best asset protection and shielding from litigation, and in addition, the NEHTrust™ provides:

1. A legitimate *"takeover"* of one's existing loan payments, without loan assumption or violation of the underlying lender's alienation and "due-on-sale" admonitions.[7]

2. A higher 'selling price' in most instances. In view of the benefits derived by the offeror, a NEHTrust's *Mutually Agreed Value* ("MAV") is typically higher than a standard "purchase offer" wherein a significant reduction in the asking price is almost universally expected. NEHTrust™ buyers typically expect to pay a premium in order to avoid the penalties of marginal cash and credit issues.

6

3.   A faster sale and shorter escrow, since there is no waiting-period for loan application, qualification and approval.

4.   Avoidance of the IRS' imposition of income tax on *Debt-Relief* (with reference to one's authorized disposition of an over-encumbered property at less than is owed to the bank) when foreclosure or "short-sale"[8] are the considered options. The NEHTrust™ seller simply does not need to destroy his/her credit and walk away with nothing to show for all those years of expense and hard work (see #10 below).

5.   Freedom from loan payments which may no longer be affordable, as well as the costs of insurance and general maintenance—since such costs are [generally] paid entirely by the NEHTrust's resident co-beneficiary.

6.   Enhanced income and profit potential, compared to what *renting* or *leasing* could provide. The structure of the NEHTrust™ eliminates or at least ameliorates one's negative cash flow, management costs, maintenance and vacancies.

7.   The ability of the homeowner to transfer income tax benefits and other benefits of ownership. For a landlord, gross rental income is most often increased by 125 to 150 percent (or can even be doubled in many cases), while *net* rental profits are frequently multiplied by 100 or 1,000 (or more) percent, due simply to one's elimination of the costs of management, maintenance, repairs, property taxes and insurance.

8.   Protection from possible injurious or malevolent actions of the "other party,' due to the recourse and tough penalties built into the system (e.g., a resident's nonpayment, disrepair, disregard or vandalism of the property).

9. In comparison with traditional *seller-carry* (OWC) arrangement, a shielding of the property from an errant party's tax liens, lawsuits, bankruptcy, judgment liens, probate and power-struggles in marital dissolution.

10. The easiest collection of a resident's payments; handling of disbursements to creditors; mailing of late notices; and processing any necessary admonitions, evictions or other legal processes—the seller need never handle these functions.[9]

11. Ease of eviction and avoidance of the time, anguish and expense of *judicial foreclosure, ejectment* and *quiet title* actions to regain entry and possession following a tenant/buyer's default. A prominent advantage of the NEHTrust™ over typical seller-assisted financing is that it always allows for a standard simple eviction and unlawful detainer process rather than foreclosure being the only recourse, as is indeed the case with *contracts for deed, equity shares, wraparound mortgages, lease-purchase* arrangements, etc.

12. Partition of the profit potential to be derived from a future sale, while, in the meantime, *someone else* pays all the bills. In negotiation a NEHTrust™ seller *(nonresident settlor beneficiary)* could bargain to retain—along with any beginning equity held—a percentage of the property's future profit potential from appreciation, improvements and mortgage principal reduction. The justification for such participation might simply be one's having been the party who obtained the original loan; the one who has made the original down payment; and/or perhaps, just for being the one who is remaining *at risk* [re: the continuing primary mortgage responsibility].[10]

Benefits for the Investor

When acquiring investment real estate, one's goal in most, if not all cases is to maximize profits by striving for the lowest purchase price, the least cash expended, the best cash flow, the lowest management and maintenance costs, and the fastest and least stressful process, from offer to close.

It is in this regard in particular that the NEHTrust™ shines for investors, especially for those who may be a bit *cash, credit and income challenged*. Here are but a few of the many benefits afforded real estate investors (with or without cash and credit) who have taken the time to learn, understand and utilize the NEHTrust™ Transfer.

1.   Safe real estate acquisition with no or minimal down payment.

2.   Avoidance (frequently) of credit checks.

3.   Avoidance of bank loan applications and the approval process.

4.   Convenient and legitimate loan payment takeover without undue compromise of a lender's due-on-sale admonitions.

5.   The ability to control a property and its revenue without publicly announcing ownership of it.

6.   The ability to shield one's real estate assets from public view, and/or from scrutiny by would-be claimants and their attorneys in legal actions.

7.   The ability to transfer income tax benefits to tenant/buyers for higher monthly revenues and total freedom from management and maintenance responsibilities and expense.

9

8. The ability to have a free property manager in every income property (the co-beneficiary tenant/buyer).

9. The ability to evict an errant tenant/buyer as a straight lease tenant, rather than risking a claim by a tenant of his/her possessing "equity," which trick is often used by defaulting tenant/buyers to thwart the eviction process, force a time-consuming judicial foreclosure, and bring about an ejectment action in order to buy time and months of free rent.

10. The ability to keep real estate ownership off one's credit and/or mortgage loan application.

11. The ability to avoid "dealer status" while controlling and acquiring large numbers of properties.

12. The ability to avoid seasoning and double-escrow issues when buying *wholesale* and selling *retail* ("flipping").

13. The ability to obtain all the objectives of any creative, seller-assisted financing arrangement (lease, option, lease-purchase, rent-to-own, wrap, contract for deed, equity share, etc.) with none of their many risks and downsides.

General Features

Ease of Dealing with Default: In the event of default, eviction of a defaulting NEHTrust™ resident beneficiary bypasses the costly and arduous processes of *foreclosure*, in that the resident's ownership rights are limited by the trust to a personal property beneficial interest in the trust that holds the property's title, rather than in the real property itself.

In essence, a defaulting resident beneficiary can be treated strictly as only *a tenant in default of its lease of the property;* rather than as a defaulting owner of real estate. For example, in the event of nonpayment, such default can be met with a *Notice-to-Pay-or-Quit,* and, if necessary, an *Unlawful Detainer Action.* From the inception of the NEHTrust™, all parties agree that any uncured default will result in:

A) eviction,

B) revocation of the trust, and

C) a return of the property to the non-defaulting beneficiaries.[11]

Income Tax Deferment: Because the NEHTrust™ constitutes a divestiture of personal property (personalty) rather than of real estate (realty), the parties settle on a *"Mutually Agreed Value"* at inception, rather than on a *"selling price."* A *sales price* per se is, therefore, not established until the actual disposition of the property when the trust terminates up to twenty-one years later. As a result of there being no actual *real estate sale,* income tax that would otherwise be due upon transfer of title and possession, can be deferred until the termination of the NEHTrust™ and the actual disposition of the real property held by the trust.

Upon disposition of the property at the scheduled trust termination date, tax on capital gain can of course be even further deferred by exchanging one's interest in the trust for other investment real estate (or for interest in another land trust) under IRC §1031 *Like-Kind Tax Deferred Exchange* guidelines.[12]

Limited Title Transfer and Title Involvement: The legal and equitable title to a property placed in a NEHTrust™ passes only to the trustee for the underlying land trust. Since the land trust is beneficiary-directed, it does thereby remain under the original owner's exclusive direction until another successor beneficiary is appointed.

Following the conveyance of title to the trustee, the trust property itself can be *leased* to a would be *buyer; there*after, the *lessee,* in order to effectively obtain the benefits and incidents of *homeownership,* need only be given a *co-beneficiary* status in the mortgagor's land trust.

Whether the property is leased first, with beneficial interest being conveyed later, or beneficial interest is conveyed first and the property occupied later, is unimportant, so long as the trust itself is legitimately established in advance of either of these secondary events.

Anonymity: Except for the original owner's conveyance of title to the third-party (hopefully *corporate*) trustee, the trust and all related NEHTrust™ documents are never placed into public record (i.e., not *"recorded"*). Furthermore, the trustee for a title-holding land trust is exempt from any requirement to reveal information about the trust, or the identity of its beneficiaries to *anyone.* [13]

Current Property Taxes Remain Unchanged: Because the land trust (that is the basis for the NEHTrust™ transfer) is an inter-vivos (*living)* trust, conveyance of property to its trustee does not constitute a taxable sale or divestiture of real property. And since no profit, or recognized gain takes place by transferring "bare" legal title to a title-holding land trust, there is no basis (e.g., purchase price) upon which to base a tax. This means that the current property tax assessment basis can remain unchanged. Each subsequent unrecorded assignment of beneficiary interest or leasehold interest is an assignment solely of personalty and, therefore, not normally subject to transfer taxation or alteration in a property's tax assessment basis.[14]

1. Show Up
2. Pay Attention
3. Be Honest
4. Stay Unassociated
   with the End-Result

The Power is in not being attached to the outcome.

Bill Gatten

A Fortune in Free Real Estate

TWO

OK, WE'RE READY.
JUST WHAT IS A "TRUST" ANYWAY?
LET'S START THERE...

Trusts, or *trust arrangements*, in their many forms have been in common use throughout the world for centuries.[15] They are structured by their creators (settlors) to accomplish an unending variety of objectives for the parties involved: business dealings, asset protection, tax savings, privacy, gifting of monies, intestate (after death) holding and/or distribution of assets, emulations of partnership and corporate structures, etc. For our purposes, here, however, we will be dealing only with the title-holding trust model known (in all U.S. states) as the *Illinois land trust.*

Within itself, a *trust* of any kind is an agreement between parties wherein one of them is en[*trust*]ed with the ownership of an asset, or group of assets (e.g., money, jewels, real property, or perhaps one's entire estate or business) for the *benefit* of others. The *Illinois land trust* is a special kind of trust designed specifically for holding, and making private, the title to real estate.

Terminology: Commonly, the party creating the trust, and placing its assets into it, is referred to as:

1)   the *trustor* (relative to "trusting someone") but is also called

2)   the *grantor* (relative to the "granting of ownership") and as

15

3)   the **settlor** (relative to having formed or created the trust, "*the donor of a settlement*"). [16]

The party that is given, and who accepts, the responsibility of ownership and most often (though not in a land trust) management of the assets in trust is the **trustee** (i.e., the trusted party). In the *land trust* all such management responsibilities fall to the beneficiaries, not to the trustee.

The party, or parties who are to receive the *benefit* deriving from the asset/s held *in trust* are referred to as **the beneficiary** or **the beneficiaries.**

The document that spells out each of the party's responsibilities to the trust, the property, and to each other, is referred to simply as **the trust,** or the **trust agreement.**

Any asset being placed into the trust (i.e., "funding" the trust) is referred to as the trust's **res** (Latin for "thing").

By relinquishing ownership of *a thing* to a trusted party, but retaining its *benefit,* a trust's beneficiaries can enjoy the use of the asset, while avoiding some of the disadvantages that could be associated with its *ownership:* such disadvantages might include legal exposure; excessive or redundant income taxation; personal liability; or simply public knowledge of one's personal affairs. In other words, a trust can be seen as a legal means for separating the *ownership* of an asset from its *possession, use* and *enjoyment.*

In most types of trusts, the party that is designated or nominated as the trustee is the party who directs and administers the trust, and manages the assets held by it. Any trust so managed and/or *directed* by its trustee is referred to as being **"trustee-directed"** vs. being grantor-directed or beneficiary-directed (the *land* *trust,* with which we are most concerned, is **beneficiary-directed**).

Anyone choosing to have absolute control over, and management of, a trust, must name him/herself as the trustee in a trustee-directed trust, or as the beneficiary in a beneficiary-directed trust, or as the grantor in a simple grantor's trust.

The last type of trust, the Grantor's Trust is considered "dry" and without any real force or effect other than avoidance of probate proceedings upon the death of the grantor. It is commonly referred to as a *Family Living Trust* or a *Fully Funded Inter Vivos Family Trust.*

The land trust model at the center of the NEHTrust™ system and this book, is wholly *beneficiary-directed.* In other words, a land trust trustee appointed (nominated) by the beneficiaries can be instructed to hold a property's title in its own name and, solely at the direction of the beneficiaries, be instructed to sell the property at a future date. During the term of the trust, the land trust trustee remains fully responsible to, and is directed exclusively by, its beneficiary/ies. Such direction is made either unanimously by all beneficiaries, or the beneficiaries can elect to appoint one among them as the sole director of the trust and manager of the trust property.

The Grantor Trust

The simple trust form known as the *"grantor trust,"* if properly drawn, effectively retains all authority and power of direction with the party who created the trust (the "grantor"), which party generally serves simultaneously as the trustee and the only beneficiary. Such a simple trusts has little if any actual value from standpoints of anonymity, asset protection or transfer of true benefit to another party. The IRS, for example, would characterize income tax benefits in a grantor trust as accruing solely to the grantor, rather than to second or third co-beneficiary/ies,[17] contrary to the objectives of the land trust.

CAUTION

Some individuals, in an attempt to emulate NARS' success, without its background, knowledge base, legal resources or experience, do knowingly use the described *grantor's trust* model rather than the Illinois land trust in an attempt to accomplish the objectives of the NARS Equity Holding Trust™ System, thereby seriously compromising the protections afforded by it.

For example, a land trust trustee must charge a fee, and a collection entity must not charge a fee; the trustee's name must come first on title, the trustee must have duties; etc., to mention but a few out of hundreds of special nuances. It is these myriad special (and little known) characteristics of the land trust that allow the system to function as simply, flawlessly and safely as it does, while withstanding the close scrutiny of lenders, the courts and the IRS since 1993. (NARS' predecessor, Resource Management Services, was established in 1984).

There are no companies, organizations or individuals licensed by North American Realty Services, Inc. to provide a product or service that is the same as, or similar to, the proprietary copyrighted and trademarked NARS NEHTrust™

"Doing for a brief while what others are UNWILLING TO DO, means being able to charge for a lifetime for that which others are UNABLE TO DO"

Anonymous

A Fortune in Free Real Estate

THREE

AGAIN...HOW DOES THE *LAND TRUST* DIFFER FROM OTHER TRUST FORMS?

Within itself, the title-holding [Illinois-type] land trust is a simple and convenient way to position the title to real estate so as to eliminate many of the difficulties associated with real estate ownership, acquisition, management and disposition.

As discussed earlier, some of the many benefits of holding real estate in a land trust include: privacy and anonymity of ownership; protection from undue estate taxation upon the death of an owner; simplification of probate administration; convenience in estate planning; protection of the corpus (the property) from lawsuits, judgment creditor liens, tax liens, bankruptcy and litigation in marital or partnership dissolution.

Even the **IRS** cannot penetrate a properly constructed land trust that names a successor beneficiary or remainder agent (the party designated to assume management in the event of the death of the primary beneficiary).

In use throughout the United States for more than 75 years,[18] the land trust, which is the underpinning of the *NEHTrust™ System,* was originally modeled from what has been popularly referred to as the "Massachusetts Business Trust."

Overall, the land trust is characterized as an *express* (written), *inter vivos* (i.e., "living")[19] *revocable, beneficiary-directed* real estate title-holding trust.

21

In the land trust model, a designated [preferably corporate] third-party trustee holds both the legal and equitable title[20] to the res of the trust (the real estate).

Since the land trust property's legal and equitable titles are not, therefore, held by the trust's beneficiaries, creation of the trust and the vesting of property's title with the trustee has the effect, under most state's laws, of having converted one's ownership of real property (realty) to ownership of personal property (personalty). This is true even though the IRS characterizes beneficiary interest in the "Illinois-type" land trust as ownership of real estate for all federal income tax purposes...assuming the tax payer holds at least a ten percent interest in the trust. [21]

Contrary to the structure of other trust forms, land trust beneficiaries direct the trustee in all matters relative to title ownership and the property's disposition throughout its term of the agreement. Even though the land trust trustee is the undisputed legal owner of the trust property, beyond holding the property's title and conducting the disposition of the property (at the direction of the beneficiaries), it generally has no other function, powers, legal rights, obligations, or responsibilities, though it can be directed to sign legal documents and apply for loans at the beneficiary's direction.

Throughout its history, the land trust's primary purpose has been to provide its beneficiaries a practical (and anonymous) alternative form of real estate possession, use and disposition—which is to say that one may own a property by acquiring the deed itself, or may instead own a beneficiary interest in a land trust whose trustee holds the legal and equitable title to the property (See IRC §163(h)4(D).

Perhaps one of the more significant differences between the *land trust* and other trust types is that (assuming there are two or more unrelated beneficiaries),[22] any real estate vested in the land trust trustee is functionally protected from creditor claims, tax liens, and virtually all other legal actions.

This *legal shielding* of the property comes about as the result of the relative *non-partitionable* nature of personal property. In other words, since co-owned personalty can't ordinary be partitioned to satisfy a creditor's judgment against one beneficiary alone, a creditor dealing with a single co-beneficiary of the trust is forced to proceed in its action solely against the individual without being able to access the trust property (i.e. legally speaking, "*in personam* rather than "*in rem*").[23]

Still another unique feature of the land trust, which is not shared by many other trust forms, is that the land trust affords its beneficiaries what is known as *reversionary benefit* or avoidance of *reversionary penalty.*" This is to say that, irrespective of how much a property may appreciate during the trust's term: when the trust terminates, or is revoked, and the title is transferred back to the settlor, the transfer is not taxed.[24]

Once again, the assignment or sale of beneficial interest in a land trust remains *private, anonymous and unrecorded;* and the ownership is of personal estate (*not* real estate). It is also for these reasons that when a successor beneficiary (rather than a replacement beneficiary) is added to a land trust, a lender's legal right to call the underlying mortgage due and payable, because of a "transfer of, or change in, ownership," is not invoked.[25] The assignment of beneficial interest in a land trust (e.g., appointment of a remainder agent or successor beneficiary) is no less valid or binding if written on the back of a paper napkin (in lipstick)—assuming that such an assignment would contain the elements of a contract,[26] and the trustee is duly notified of it.

A land trust's beneficiaries (if each agrees), may easily transfer, gift, giveaway, borrow-against or exchange their respective beneficiary interests without undue income tax penalty, and without imperiling the property's title.

Financial Success and real Wealth
are as different from one another
as are owning an airplane and
having the ability to fly it.

Bill Gatten

A Fortune in Free Real Estate

FOUR

SO, HOW DOES ALL THIS STUFF COME TOGETHER IN THE NARS EQUITY HOLDING TRUST™?

First off, it must be clearly understood that the *NEHTrust™* in itself is not a trust: it is instead an ownership transfer mechanism that utilizes a land trust at its basis. It is a carefully constructed combination of documents that create a legal conveyance from one person to another of virtually all the benefits of a traditional home sale or purchase, but without a title transfer beyond the nominated trusted entity (the trustee). The basic documents making up the NEHTrust™ Transfer, which will be discussed in detail later in the book, are: the *Land Trust,* an *Assignment of Beneficiary Interest,* a *Beneficiary Agreement* between parties, and a triple net *Occupancy Agreement* wherein the tenant beneficiary is required to cover all recurring costs of ownership.

The basis for the structure and use of the NEHTrust™ Transfer System stem partially from the fact that the federal tax code allows an income tax deduction for mortgage interest and property tax for qualified property owners and residents of real property who are able to demonstrate the following:

1) Having the risks and burdens of ownership;

2) The property being their primary residence;

3) Having a contractual obligation to pay the related mortgage interest and property taxes;

and..

4) That the tax payer also possesses either –

    a) an *equitable interest* in the property, or
    b) a *beneficiary interest* in an *estate or [land] trust* that holds the equitable title to the property.[27]

Put another way, federal *"qualified property"* requirements for residential income tax deduction (re. mortgage interest and property tax) specifically declare that in order for an individual to claim an income tax write-off for residential mortgage interest and property tax:

- The payor must be contractually obligated to pay mortgage-interest and property tax amounts (e.g., as directed within the NARS Equity Holding Trust's Occupancy Agreement)

- The payor must have a contractual conveyance of ownership executed by parties (e.g., via an "Assignment of Beneficial Interest")

- The payments being made must be for the payor's principal and primary residence (e.g., as are appropriately reflected in an interrelated "Occupancy Agreement")

- The payor must be contractually bound to bear the ordinary rewards, risks, and burdens of homeownership expense, and potential for monetary loss (i.e., the "risk and burden of possession") as described in an interrelated Beneficiary Agreement, as well as in the Occupancy Agreement

- The payor must be able to demonstrate that he/she holds either —

    a) an equitable interest in the qualified residence (which NEHTrust beneficiaries do not)...or

    b) a beneficial interest in a trust or estate that holds equitable interest in the qualified residence [28] (...as per the land trust agreement, this interest is created prior to the structuring of the NEHTrust™, and is transferred by the subsequent Beneficiary Agreement)

A seller's decision to place a troublesome property into a land trust and form a 2 or 3 party NEHTrust™ transfer can bring fresh air and a welcome reprieve from the discomforts of trying to get out from under the heavy burden of an unwanted property.[29]

The next step is then identifying a competent would-be resident beneficiary who, in exchange for all the benefits of homeownership, would agree to pay all (or most) of the property's recurring costs, including mortgage-interest, property tax and maintenance expenses.

Or...one might opt to deal with a *real estate investor* who would step in and take over as the trust's *remainder co-beneficiary* and assume the primary responsibility for all costs: payments, property tax, insurance, maintenance and repairs...in anticipation of future profits (e.g., from appreciation, mortgage principal reduction and/or an ongoing cash flow from the management and rental of the property).

As is probably quite evident by now, virtually all the benefits of home ownership can be conveyed to an acquiring party via the NEHTrust™, without the necessity of new financing and without the standard down-payment requirement. Moreover, for any seller willing to remain responsible for the existing mortgage "for a while," the NEHTrust™ conveniently and significantly diminishes costs and risks of a standard purchase arrangement and/or standard disposition costs, especially when compared to any other so-called creative *seller-assisted financing* arrangement.

Other legally volatile and risky *creative financing* alternatives can be easily avoided while also avoiding the expense and resultant credit damage so often associated with so-called "wraparound mortgages," *rental or leasing* of residential property, *lease/purchase-options, land contracts, equity shares, 'short-sales (i.e. the Offer and Compromise)'* or relinquishment to a lender's foreclosure. One's selling or acquiring homeownership benefits via the NEHTrust™, is often singularly the most logical and conservative alternative to the traditional real estate transfer.

Hoping, Wishing and Praying are the tools of gamblers and supplicants. Isolating your needs and trusting in your God to fulfil them, and knowing for sure that it will happen, is all that's ever needed.

Bill Gatten

A Fortune in Free Real Estate

FIVE
THE AGREEMENT AND FINAL DISPOSITION OF THE PROPERTY. WHAT HAPPENS AT TERMINATION?

The NEHTrust's™ related *Beneficiary Agreement* stipulates that, at the trust's termination (in from, say, 1 to 21 years or at the end of any mutually agreed-upon term, which can be as long as the length of the underlying mortgage financing), the trustee shall offer the property for sale at the *then* Fair-Market-Value.

Following retirement of all debt against the property, and after a return of each beneficiary's initial contribution (e.g., equity carried by settlor or investor; initial nonrecurring closing costs expended by any beneficiary), the net proceeds of sale are then distributed between (or *among*) the beneficiaries in proportion to their respective percentages of beneficiary interest held (e.g., 50-50 or 50-40-10 or 90-10 or 50-25-25; etc.).

The NEHTrust™ Beneficiary Agreement allows that beneficiary residing in the property at termination the first right to buy or refinance the property and assume its full ownership. If over the trust's term, the property fails to appreciate enough to allow for a profitable sale, then the parties may mutually agree to extend the agreement for another period; [31] or, should the resident so choose, he/she could simply vacate the property, allowing its return to the nonresident co-beneficiary or to the settlor beneficiary (the original owner) without further obligation.

In a 3-party NEHTrust (settlor, investor and resident), unless stipulated otherwise in the documentation, the first right to purchase at termination goes to the resident beneficiary; the second right is to the investor beneficiary, and the final right to purchase goes to the original owner (settlor beneficiary).

In order to avoid creation of a *"predetermined buy-out,"* a *"bargain purchase price,"* a *"purchase option,"* or a *"disguised mortgage loan" per se* (each of which could invoke unfavorable treatment by the IRS and the courts), the parties agree, within the Beneficiary Agreement, that the *sale-price* at termination will be the property's true fair-market-value (FMV) as is to be established by a bona-fide appraisal. [32]

Should the resident beneficiary opt at termination to refinance and purchase the trust property, then all equity, appreciation, and principal reduction having accrued on his/her behalf, will be deducted from such FMV purchase price prior to any other distributions of proceeds. At that time, the other nonresident beneficiaries must be [re]paid any equity they may have possessed at the beginning of the NEHTrust™ prior to the final distributin of net proceeds.

When you're plagued with a fear that someone is doing something bad behind your back...most often all you need to do is turn around and look.

Bill Gatten

A Fortune in Free Real Estate

SIX

A MOST LOGICAL APPROACH TO THE INTENT, OBJECTIVES AND END-RESULTS OF *ALL OTHER* "CREATIVE FINANCING" TECHNIQUES ...WITHOUT THEIR DOWNSIDES

For those who understand the land trust and its myriad features and regulations relative to it, the *NEHTRUST™* is an exemplary means of real property disposition, acquisition and management, especially when compared to virtually *any currently* known *creative (seller-assisted) financing* techniques.

The fact is that the NEHTrust™ within itself is *not* an *alternative* to these other financing schemes (wraparound, contract for deed, equity share, purchase options and the like). It is instead simply the way to meet the intent and objectives of these other, too often, risky and volatile (albeit, sometimes *quite clever*) devices.

The following is a brief descriptive list of a few of these "other" potentially risky and less prudent "creative" attempts to relieve the stress of unwanted, or no longer affordable, real estate.

Although not particularly novel within themselves, this list includes the foreclosure and the *offer-and-compromise* (mortgage debt forgiveness in lieu of foreclosure, commonly known as the "short-sale") as means for ridding oneself of the burden of an unwanted, un-affordable or unmanageable property.

Short Sale (the *Offer and Compromise*)

The prospect of *debt-forgiveness* may sound like a blessing in a time-of-need...until the person being so "blessed" suddenly realizes that in order to qualify for the right to walk away from an onerous or over-encumbered property, he/she must prove themselves to be virtually insolvent financially, and be willing to allow total destruction of their credit worthiness for years to come (more than it may already have been damaged),[34] and they must also have procured a ready and willing qualified buyer.

Then comes the next sudden insight...that any debt forgiveness by the lender ("debt relief") is fully taxable as ordinary income; and that the tax bill is due and payable in the year the debt-relief "windfall" is realized (e.g., were one to be in, say, a 33% tax bracket, $50,000 in debt-forgiveness can result in almost $17,000 in unexpected tax being levied...and tax debt is not avoidable by filing bankruptcy).

To top it all off, when the smoke clears, the "forgiven debtor" ends up empty-handed, having lost his/her home, and having been forced to walk away with nothing to show for the original down-payment, all those years of payments, hard work, self-sacrifice and effort. This is especially problematic when it is realized that all the while, there were virtually thousands of would-be buyers who would gladly have taken over the payments—perhaps even for just the tax benefits alone, via an Equity Holding Trust™ transfer—thus saving the day (plus recovering lots of lost dollars and saving one's credit standing).

Foreclosure

Many overburdened homeowners erroneously reason that if they are willing to sacrifice their credit standing, they can just "walk away" from a burdensome property without further repercussions. The fact is, however, that not unlike the foregoing short-sale scenario, unless the defaulting borrower can prove insolvency, the difference between what is owed to the lender and what the property is finally sold for, is reported to the IRS, and treated, along with the lender's administrative expenses and costs of disposition, as imminently taxable income ("debt-relief").

The IRS 'may' also treat any unpaid ("back") mortgage interest as taxable windfall income to the defaulting party as well.

Deed-in-Lieu (of Foreclosure)

The "DIL" is a transfer document that can ostensibly be presented to a mortgagee (lender) in hopes of avoiding the process of being officially foreclosed upon (i.e.: "Help, don't hurt me! I'll freely deed the property to you...here, take it! Please!).

Although a wholly valid and enforceable transfer device, in a slow, declining or stagnant real estate market a lender's willingness to accept ownership of a property by a deed in lieu of foreclosure is highly improbable (...an understatement). A lenders's acceptance of such a non-performing property would place the transferee (the lender) in a position of responsibility for all unpaid property taxes, mortgage payments and insurance premiums. As a result, such a lender in possession would likely be unable to pass off these expenses via the filing of a Form 1099 with the IRS on behalf of their defaulted borrower.

But, be all this as it may, stories continue to abound about homeowners giving DIL's to their mortgage lenders, then quickly running down to the court house to record it in the public record, only to learn that not only does the bank continue with the foreclosure process, but it also can refuse to relinquish the forfeited deed should the money to reinstate the loan become available at the last minute. This obviously puts a pretty good crimp in any alternatives the buyer in default may have had before *going off half-cocked* (as it were).

However, in view of these facts, even when a lender entertains acceptance of such a transfer, they make certain that the IRS views any resulting debt-relief and/or unpaid amounts (e.g., back payments, insurance, property taxes, etc.) as fully taxable to the transferor[35] in order to avoid being financially liable for it themselves.

Do note that some self-proclaimed creative real estate investment pundits have been known to blindly (and stupidly) proclaim to large audiences that one way to circumvent a lender's due-on-sale admonitions in the face of a non-assumable loan, is to create a phony promissory note and junior mortgage for, say, $100, with the property owner as the payor and the acquiring party as the payee. The holder of the note is to then fake a foreclosure for nonpayment by the former homeowner. At this point the naive assumption is that the holder of the fake note can avoid the due-on-sale clause in the mortgage by servicing the first mortgage with impunity and without the first mortgagee's consent or involvement.

As logical as it could sound to some, *do not try this at home!* Such a scheme will definitely not deprive any lender of its right to foreclose relative to an unauthorized transfer, and will more than likely fan their low-salary/high impact *authority flame*. And, too, such a trick could also open the way for the once (but no longer) "over-the-barrel" owner to come back later and claim that unconscionable advantage had been taken of him in his time of duress: thereupon demanding, and likely receiving, a return of his real estate along with some big bucks for liquidated and punitive damages from the unwary investor.

Lease-Option

Though it always seems unlikely to many, a lease option ("L/O") is distinctly a violation of any lender's due-on-sale clause (state, federal or private)...whether the option is recorded or not. If unrecorded, neither party has any protection against untoward actions of the other. And when it is recorded, it can severely cloud a property's title, as well as invite the underlying mortgage holder to *call* its loan due and payable—requiring, of course, immediate payment in full of the entire remaining balance of the mortgage.[36]

In the L/O the interests of the *optionor* and *optionee* are jeopardized in other ways as well. For example, as we said, *recording* a lease option clouds the title and therefore violates the lender's alienation provisions, while *not* recording it exposes the optionee to an unscrupulous optionor's commission of fraud and/ or deception. This is to say, that a *recorded* document will most often take precedence over an unrecorded one. This means that the option, or the property itself, could be granted (sold) or lease-optioned to an unknowing buyer or other optionee, despite the existence of the otherwise valid contract. And the individual in the unrecorded transaction usually, thought not always, loses to the party with the publicly recorded deed.

41

Far more often than is generally realized, desperate lease optionors (who tend to look and act *real honest* on first meeting) frequently do, in fact, over-encumber lease-optioned properties without the knowledge of the optionee. Usually an optionor's borrowing against the property in excess of the agreed-upon option strike price does this. And, too, optionors are known to engage [frequently] in still other devious actions that can cause liens and judgments to silently attach to the lease-optioned property unbeknownst to the tenant, until an attempt to exercise the option is made.

From the optionor's (owner's) standpoint, as any seasoned landlord will attest, attempting to evict a defaulting optionee, who alleges immunity from eviction due to a claim of possessing "Equity (i.e., an *equitable interest* in the leased property)" can become extremely financially burdensome and time-consuming. The cry most often heard in court from the poor and sorely abused tenant in possession is usually one of having "Equity." In other words, the tenant claims that because of having paid an option fee or "rent credits" that were to apply to a future purchase of the property, he or she is no longer a tenant, but is now an equity holder (an owner) and, therefore, immune to eviction.

This state of affairs (when an equity claim is made) invariably forces a judicial foreclosure process, which can be expensive, exhausting, nerve-racking, time-consuming...and often even a *futile exercise*. This is because more often than not, the tenant prevails at the unlawful detainer hearing, forcing the property owner into a full judicial foreclosure and an *ejectment* process (i.e., in order to reclaim a right of entry and possession). And sadly, while the cash draining brouhaha continues week-after-week and month-after-month, the optionee stays put...obstructing the re-marketing or re-letting of the property and living completely rent-free, at the owner's expense while his/her attorney works on a *contingency basis (i.e.,* the tenant's attorney receives no payment until the case is won or settled out of court) knowing full well that if it can be stretched-out long enough, the claimant will cave-in and settle rather than continuing a losing battle. All the while, the landlord has to pay—*through the nose* —for his/her legal counsel while the tenant's lawyer works for free.

Even if the landlord were to continue the fight for the sake of *principle,* the only reward to be enjoyed would be that of getting rid of the tenant (...after they've likely taken a baseball bat to the windows on their way out). Either way the tenant wins, either by receiving moving expenses and months of free rent: or by being handed a free house, should the judgment actually turn out to be against the landlord...and sometimes it does.

So, what are the downsides of the Lease Option that can be avoided via the use of the NEHTrust™? And will it provide the same intended end results?

- An option to purchase violates a lenders' due-on-sale clause (See USC §1701-j-3): whereas *when there is no sale, and only a lease of the property for less than three years and without an option to purchase, there can be no due-on-sale violation.* That is the Equity Holding Trust Transfer.

- An optionee successfully claiming an "equity interest" in the leased property by virtue of having received rent credits and having paid an option fee (i.e., when such is to later apply to the purchase price), and who therefore cannot be evicted for nonpayment, forcing a costly and time-

43

consuming judicial foreclosure and possible ejectment and quiet-title action; *whereas an Equity Holding Trust™ co-beneficiary leasing the property, even though with full "benefits' of ownership, has no de facto ownership in the realty, and can therefore be evicted as would be any defaulting rental tenant.*

- If an optionee's claim of "Equity" does have foundation, the tenant's creditor liens, lawsuits, judgments, bankruptcies, tax liens, marital dispute litigation and probate can seriously impair the title and prevent a sale; *whereas use of the co-beneficiary land trust disallows attachment and charging orders against the property by judgment creditors.*

- All too frequently, and too easily, optionors change their minds about the optionee's right to purchase when a property's value increases dramatically over time; *whereas a co-beneficiary land trust works like an ongoing Escrow, in that no party can make a decision or give a direction to the trustee (the property's titleholder) unless there is unanimous agreement.*

- Dishonest optionors all too frequently and too easily over-encumber or cloud the title to optioned properties without the knowledge of the optionee: *whereas such actions are excluded by virtue of the mutual (unanimous) power of direction requirement within the Equity Holding Trust. ™*

Land-Sale Contract (Also known as a "Land Contract," "Contract for Sale," "Contract for Deed," or "Contract for Mortgage")

Besides often unwittingly creating a forfeiture of a seller's IRC §1031 tax-deferment privileges,[38] so-called "land contracts" remain clear violations of any lender's due-on-sale clause. Perhaps equally important, however, is the fact that in the absence of an actual *purchase agreement* (i.e., a Contract *"For"* Sale, which conveys *equitable interest*) a "buyer's" income tax deduction for interest and property tax will be denied. And like most other *creative financing* arrangements, land sale contracts often fail to protect the buyer, or to provide the seller adequate remedy in the face of default, damage, disrepair, neglect or abandonment of the property.

As is true with all of the forgoing financing *schemes*, illicit acts of a devious 'seller' can, and *often do*, seriously injure the interests of innocent land contract buyers. Likewise, honest, well meaning, but unwary, sellers can be equally vulnerable to a defaulting buyer's negligence, illicit and illegal acts and/or refusal to leave the property, even when payments are not being made (legitimately claiming "equity" in the property). And, as in virtually all "creative financing" schemes, any divorce disputes, liens, suits, bankruptcies, or other legal actions, by or against either of the parties–resident or non-resident–are likely to seriously imperil the title, and therefore the interests of the "other" party.

What's wrong with a Contract for Deed (aka: "CFD," Land Contract, Land Sale Contract, etc.) that can be avoided by the use of the NEHTrust™, while accomplishing the same objective and end-result?

- For starters the CFD directly violates a lenders' due-on-sale clause: *the NEHTrust does not.*

- The "vendee (acquiring party)" cannot be evicted for nonpayment, resulting in costly and time-consuming foreclosure (one cannot evict an owner): *the resident co-beneficiary in a land trust, on the other hand, is never an owner of the property per se, and therefore, remains subject to eviction.*

- A CFD buyer's creditor liens, lawsuits, judgments, bankruptcies, tax liens, marital dispute litigation and probate can seriously attach to and cloud the property's title: *such liens cannot attach to a property owned by a co-beneficiary land trust.*

- A CFD buyer's poor payment record can be reflected on the vendor's (seller's) credit report for years to come: *in the NEHTrust, a Contingency Fund for slow payment and eviction assures that lender payments are made promptly.*

- With a CFD, title does not pass to the vendee until the property is fully paid for, and unless the contract is constructed as a true Contract of Sale (conveying equitable interest) per se, tax benefits are denied for the vendee: *in the NEHTrust™ all income tax benefits are available from day-one, as are all other benefits of home ownership.*

- Federal and state tax liens attach to a contract for deed property; *this is not so with a property held by a co-beneficiary land trust.*

The "Subject-To"

The term *subject-to* is a generic expression used to describe virtually any of the aforementioned surreptitious "creative financing" arrangements wherein an owner turns a property over to another and, if equity exists, 'carries' a promissory note for it. A seller's security in such an arrangement could be a mortgage and promissory note, a trust deed and promissory note or an *All Inclusive Mortgage* (a Wrap).[37] In any such transaction, the acquiring party would be said to have accepted the transaction "subject-to" the existing terms and conditions of the original underlying financing: thus the origin of the term.

Whether seen as a serious threat or not, virtually any subject-to permutation of creative real estate financing, unless expressly authorized by the mortgagor of record, constitutes a direct violation of any lender's *due-on-sale* admonitions, allowing the lender to foreclose at will and demand that the entire loan balance be immediately paid in full (usually within no more than 90 days of discovery).

Any of these arrangements is purely and simply an unauthorized conversion of ownership of the real estate, and most certainly compromises the underlying lender's security interest in the property.

One should be forewarned that a seller in one of these transactions who would attempt to foreclose on a "new owner-of-record (i.e., the person to whom the property's title or equity was transferred)" could find the task extremely difficult, costly, time-consuming and very burdensome, if not wholly impossible. Were the lender of record to decide to resort to foreclosure to protect its interest, the former owner could not hope to protect him/herself by taking the property back and trying to undo the damage before his/her credit record was decimated.

From the buyer's point of view in such a "seller carry-back," one can never be certain that monthly obligations are being met punctually, if at all; or (if the transaction were to remain unrecorded) that income tax deductions would be allowable. Moreover, an unprincipled seller in any unrecorded financing arrangement can easily encumber the property or cloud its title without the buyer ever knowing anything about it, until its too late.

So which of these problems could the NEHTrust™ eliminate without compromising the parties' original intent and purpose?

- Again...violation of the mortgage lender's due-on-sale clause does not occur when a property is transferred to an inter vivos trust and leased out (whether to a co-beneficiary or not).

- A subject-to purchaser cannot be evicted. Costly and time-consuming judicial foreclosure is likely to become necessary, *whereas the NEHTrust™ always allows for simple eviction.*

- The acquiring party's creditor liens, lawsuits, judgments, bankruptcies, tax liens, marital dispute litigation and probate will seriously impair the title to the property, while the original borrower remains responsible for the loan and repossession for cause; however, *such actions against the property (in rem) are disallowed when the property is held in a co-beneficiary land trust.*

- A buyer's poor payment record is reflected on the seller's credit report for years to come; *whereas the NEHTrust™ provides for an ample Contingency Fund to ameliorate the effects of late payments, and provides for quick eviction of an errant "tenant-beneficiary."*

- Standard income tax penalties are applied upon consummation of the subject-to transaction, necessitating:

1) payment of taxes,

2) an IRC §121 deferment, or

3) an IRC §1031 Like-kind tax deferred exchange in order to defer or escape taxation; *whereas, in the NEHTrust™ no sale of the realty takes place for the settlor beneficiary until the end of the trust and lease term.*

The *Wrap-Around* or *"All Inclusive Mortgage"*

In a so-called *Wrap*, a seller, instead of conveying the property's title to a buyer and taking back (carrying) a second or third mortgage for his equity, can instead create an *all-inclusive mortgage* for the entire value of the property, imposing an aggregate loan payment large enough to cover all other currently existing loan payments.

In this scenario the buyer makes just one payment to the seller every month (which may also include the costs of property tax, insurance and any other assessments), which payment is usually more than sufficient to allow the seller to continue making payments on the underlying loans (say, a first and second mortgage), and to put any additional cash received in his pocket.

The Wrap-Around Mortgage (AIM/AITD), is often used as a clever ruse for obtaining a much higher interest rate than one might ordinarily pay for a second or third mortgage.

For example, let's say that a property worth $100,000 has a $50,000 first mortgage on it at 6.5%

interest, and a $30,000 second mortgage on it at 10% interest. The seller then says to a prospective buyer that he'll carry a $20,000 third mortgage for his existing equity, but that he wants 21% interest on the loan for thirty years. The buyer naturally balks at such a high interest rate, so the crafty seller says: "OK then, you got me. How about I carry the entire $100,000 for you at just 12% interest?" "Done!" says the buyer, "You got yourself a deal there!"

Now, take a moment and see which scenario would have been better for the buyer. Under the seller's first suggestion the buyer's aggregate monthly payment would have been $929.00 per-month, even with the 21% third mortgage; but under the second more "reasonable" 12% arrangement, the monthly payment is $1,129.00. Somebody just got took for $200 per-month for 30 years (that totals $72,000.00).

What is wrong with the *Wrap-Around* that can be avoided by the NEHTrust™?

- A *Wrap* clearly defies lenders' *due-on-sale* admonitions; the NEHTrust™ does not violate the clause (as long as the borrower of record remains a beneficiary).

- A Wrap buyer cannot be evicted for nonpayment. Foreclosure is therefore mandated. With the NEHTrust™ an errant resident co-beneficiary is never more than a tenant, subject to simple eviction (i.e., by prior agreement is evicted from the property and his/her interest in the trust is bought out).

- A Wrap buyer's creditor liens, lawsuits, judgments, bankruptcies, tax liens, marital dispute litigation and Probate can seriously

50

impair the title; not so with a Equity Holding Trust™.

- A Wrap buyer's poor payment record is reflected on the seller's credit report for years to come; the NEHTrust™ provides for a Contingency Fund with which to cover late payments and/or commence eviction and recovery of the property immediately...with the buyer's money.

- Recovering possession of a wrapped property in litigation could pose serious problems given that the seller is still responsible for the loan and, property taxes, insurance and any other assessments. The NEHTrust™ avoids that problem due to the ability to evict and re-market quickly.

- When a wrap, vrtually all of the seller's control of the property is given up at the close of escrow; all parties in the NEHTrust™ share a mutual (unanimous) Power of Direction over the trustee.

A Fortune in Free Real Estate

Stopping along the way to smell the roses is a good thing to do, but it won't get you off the hook for not buying some and bringing them home.

Bill Gatten

A Fortune in Free Real Estate

SEVEN
NEHTRUST STUFF THAT POPS UP FROM TIME TO TIME

Following the creation of a living trust (of any type), the appointment of a successor manager or *remainder agent* is considered prudent in order to protect the integrity of the trust in the event of the demise of the original trustee/manager of the trust and trust property. In a trustee-directed trust it is that "manager" who holds the position of *trustee*; but when the trust is *beneficiary-directed*, such as in the land trust that underpins the NEHTrust™ system, it is the beneficiary who is the manager of the trust and its property.

In a land trust in particular, multiple beneficiaries are considered necessary to best shield and protect the property from legal claims against it,[39] by virtue of the relative inability of outside judgment creditors to reach the co-owned personalty, or the trust property, for *partition* or with a *charging order* (a device used by judgment creditors to reach the assets of a single "partner" in a co-owned enterprise without harming the other partners or damaging the partnership). Such charges are not possible when the property is in a co-beneficiary land trust).

Co-owned *personal estate* (vs.. real estate), wherein its "co-owners" are unrelated and at arm's length, and therefore better able to escape attempts by a judgment creditor to *partition* the interests of the co-beneficiaries is free from threats of partition *(i.e., to "partition" an asset means to divide and sell off a parcel or portion of it in order to satisfy a claim by a judgment creditor.*

Note here that following the appointment of a *remainder (successor) beneficiary* in a land trust, the parties can mutually agree that the successor will live in, and lease the trust property from the trustee. That resident party's tenure in the property is then documented as a full-payout *("triple net")* lease agreement. This means that the co-beneficiary is now leasing from the trust in which he/she is a beneficiary, and taking on the full *risks and burdens of ownership,* although NOT taking title to, or an equitable interest in, the property (an "equity" is held only in the trust: not in the real estate).

Now...when that lease creates a contractual obligation for that person to cover all of the property's mortgage interest, property tax, insurance, and confers all the risks and burdens of ownership, the tenant/ beneficiary is (by virtue of **IRC §163(h)4(D)** entitled to the same income tax write-off for mortgage-interest and property tax that would be available to any party having acquired a home by any other means. And, too, that same party could, by a separate agreement, be given any share of future profits from appreciation, and principal reduction, that the settlor would be willing to relinquish at the trust's termination, in consideration for, say, the co-beneficiary's posting into the trust's *Contingency Fund.*

The Contingency Fund

At the inception of any NEHTrust™, it is highly recommended that one create a *Reserve Account,* referred to as "The Contingency Fund" of no less than one or two full aggregate monthly payment obligations. This reserve for contingencies can be posted (funded) by any beneficiary, or can be posted jointly by all of them. Maintained on behalf of the beneficiaries for future repairs, late payments, payment defaults, etc., this fund provides a buffer against "things that could go wrong (costs of eviction or other legal actions that could present themselves in the future)."[41]

It is strongly advised that Contingency Fund monies be maintained in a non-interest-bearing trust account, and returned in full to the party who posted the fund (if unused), less any reconveyance costs incurred, at the trust's termination.

In NARS' standard documentation, should any portion of the contingency fund be used for any reason, its replenishment is mandatory with, or prior to, the resident's next regular payment obligation. The NARS documents provide that failure to comply with this requirement can (at the discretion and direction of the nonresident beneficiaries) become reasonable cause for eviction and trust dissolution proceedings...even though the underlying mortgage payments may be current.

A Mortgagor's (Borrower's) Right to Convey Title to a Revocable Inter Vivos (Living) Trust

A borrower's right to transfer a property into a revocable, living trust in his/her name, and under his/her direction, for estate planning and income tax purposes—*without invoking the lender's right to foreclose under its due-on-sale clause*—is protected, under federal law (the *Federal Depository Institution Regulations Act of 1982*, better known as the *Garn-St. Germain Act).*[40]

This federal law also protects the right of that same borrower to lease-out the property prior to, or following, creation of the inter vivos trust, assuming that no *Option to Purchase* exists, and that the trust agreement itself contains no verbiage that would transfer *Occupancy Rights* to another, and that the trust, when created, be an inter-vivos trust, and remain *revocable by the borrower.*

Legal Shielding of The Property

When compared to more "risk laden" seller-assisted financing schemes and contrivances, the NEHTrust™, by virtue of its unique propensity for converting real property ownership to ownership of personal property, effectively protects and shields the property's title: not only hiding it from view, but when multiple beneficiaries are involved, protecting it from litigation. Consequently, the risks and hazards of creative real estate financing are greatly reduced, while investment and home ownership benefits are maximized for the buyer (resident beneficiary), the seller (nonresident beneficiary), the investor (nonresident co-beneficiary), any involved Realtor® and even the mortgage lender...whose prompt payments are ensured and backed by more than one person, and which lender's rights of foreclosure remain unaffected by the land trust and the ensuing documentation that comprises the NEHTrust.™

Characterization of Trust Ownership as *Personalty* (Personal Property)

Although treated for income tax purposes as an owner of real estate, a land trust beneficiary falls under a state's Probate and Uniform Commercial Code (UCC) regulations. The consequence of the NEHTrust™ tenant's being able to exploit income tax benefits, by virtue of being a beneficiary in a land trust that owns the property, does not impinge in any manner upon the lender's security interest. A lender may always foreclose when necessary by a legal course of action.

The NEHTrust™ is secondary to a mortgagee's (lender's) mortgage contract. This is to say that a lender can and will continue to look to the same guarantor (the borrower of record) for prompt payments and strict adherence to its loan parameters. Irrespective of the existence of the NEHTrust™ or the tenant's income tax benefits, a mortgage lender can certainly foreclose upon its security (the property), or declare its loan immediately due-and-payable, for *any* legitimate reason that is covered in its documentation, and that is within the law.

Conversion of the character of real estate ownership (by virtue of *equitable conversion*) from realty to personalty gives the land trust beneficiary the best of both worlds—the protection under state jurisdiction relating to personal property (e.g., ease of transfer and repossession, privacy, security and the ability to transfer tax benefits without a title transfer), and the benefit under federal tax law of the income tax deductions for mortgage interest and property tax.

Absence of The Need to Record

Other than the deed conveying legal title to the third-party land trust trustee, no other NEHTrust™ documents need to be placed into the public record. This includes the trust itself, the Assignment of Beneficiary Interest, the Beneficiary Agreement, the Occupancy (lease) Agreement and any limited/revocable power of attorney from one beneficiary to another.

In view of the fact that in a Land Trust a third-party fiduciary (the trustee) holds the bare legal and equitable title to the property, the recording of any document other than the transfer document (deed), itself, is not necessary to afford maximum protection for the beneficiaries.

All of the afore mentioned related documents are bona fide legal contracts, enforceable under the law. And because the trustee for the land trust is the true owner of the trust property, no beneficiary of the trust can negatively effect the other by any act that would otherwise cloud the title to the trust property.

This concept (i.e., that of holding title in this manner by a third party) can be seen as somewhat analogous to an open Escrow, wherein, because of the temporary third-party title-holding nature of the process, no involved party can effect or alter any action with respect to the property or its title without the express knowledge and unanimous consent of all parties. This is to say that: "If it's not in the contract then it can't be done...unless all parties were to be in unanimous agreement and were to so direct the trustee (in writing with certified *proof of delivery*)."

The Third-Party Collection Service and Disbursement of Funds

Utilizing the services of a responsible third party collection facility to handle the ongoing receipt and disbursement of payments can provide comfort and safety, as well as confidence for the beneficiaries.[42] Since subterfuge is not necessary with the NEHTrust,™ the collection facility (e.g., PAC Management of Los Angeles, CA, or Equity Management Services of Midpines, CA) can communicate honestly and openly with lenders, insurance companies, tax assessors, and homeowners associations with respect to all issues concerning mortgage payments, billing policies and administrative concerns or other issues that would/could arise.

The Trustee

A trustee in any land trust should be, if at all possible, a corporation, due to the fact that a corporation has *unlimited life.* Obviously, the death or incapacity of a natural person acting as trustee would unnecessarily subject the trust and its *corpus* to serious delays caused by the process of probate administration for the deceased trustee, thereby neutralizing many of the most significant advantages of the NEHTrust.™

Two Bonded Trustee Service Providers

PAC Holdings, a Nonprofit California Corporation ("PAC")

PAC has been exclusively involved in holding titles to land trust properties throughout the U.S. since 1990. Specializing in 1 and 2 beneficiary land trust transfers, the company currently holds the titles to millions of dollars worth of real estate, involving many hundreds of Equity Holding Trust™ transactions. Through its directorship and legal representation (the law firm of *Johnson, Poulsen, Coons, and Slater*, Los Angeles, CA), the company is well insured against errors, omissions, malfeasance, and legal malpractice.

At this writing the standard fee for holding title for a simple one beneficiary land trust (the single beneficiary being, say, an LLC, husband and wife, partnership, corporation, etc.) is $12.00 per month, paid annually in advance ($144.00). For multiple beneficiary long-term land trust transfers, PAC charges a onetime *Set-Up and Acceptance Fee* of $500.00 in addition to a monthly trustee holding and service fee of 0.5% per-year (half a percent) of the trust property's Mutual Agreed Value at the NEHTrust's™ inception. The trustee service fee is paid monthly along with principal, interest, taxes and insurance, as a part of the beneficiaries's aggregate recurring lease payment obligation.

The reader should note that this monthly Trustee Fee is charged as *fair compensation* for the trustee's role in, and risk of, holding title and serving as a legal buffer (and focal point of legal actions) between beneficiary and creditor, as well as for monitoring the bill-paying and collection service (PAC Management).

Equity Holding Corporation ("EHC")

EHC acts as trustee for multiple beneficiary land trust transactions (that is, three or more beneficiary entities). The members of this nonprofit corporation are all the beneficiaries of all the Equity Holding Trusts™ for whom the company holds title (all members are issued membership certificates upon acceptance of the trusteeship by EHC) and all proceeds received from trustee fees are contributed to charitable scholarship funds.

EHC is represented by counsel (the law firm of Robinson and Schmidt of Los Angles, CA) and is well insured against errors, omission, malfeasance in office and all natural hazards.

An Acceptance Fee of between $250 and $500 is charged in advance of each transaction, and a monthly trustee fee is charged (i.e.: 0.4% to 0.5% of a property's mutually agreed value at the land trust's inception).

NOTE: Although the foregoing is not intended to promote the mentioned trust companies or their bill-paying services in particular, these unaffiliated companies do pay a small consulting fee to NARS with each Equity Holding Trust™ transaction submitted to and accepted by them.

Each of the two nonprofit corporate trustees that are referred to here, and which are commonly used and recommended by NARS, has a relationship with a separate bill-paying and collections affiliate that can, at no cost to the beneficiaries, collect monthly payments and make disbursements to creditors as directed by mutual agreement of all "voting" beneficiaries. The fee paid for holding title (the *"trustee fee"*) is for trusteeship only, and is not paid to the respective collection entity. There is no fee charged by the bill-paying service (and even if another service is used, no such fee should be paid, as paying such fee could cause characterization of the entire transaction as a *homeowner's association*, being therefor double-taxed as a corporation.[43]

Further, the mentioned collection services function autonomously and remain at arms-length from NARS and the respective trustee (i.e., that is...separate in ownership, management and company structure: although funded by the trustee). The beneficiaries of each Equity Holding Trust™ transaction must manage the trust property themselves and must not pay for property management per se.

> **NOTE:** A paid collection service or property manager associated with an intended land trust would severely weaken the Trust's integrity if challenged in court or by the IRS. If the arrangement were judged to be only a partnership, corporation, business trust, disguised security agreement, homeowner's association or an equitable mortgage, virtually all of the myriad benefits and advantages of a bona fide land trust transfer would be gone. It is, therefore, important that a land trust trustee always charge a fee (commensurate with "industry standards"), and that any bill-paying entity NOT charge a fee (leaving all management in the hands of the beneficiaries). Otherwise the collections entity would be deemed a *property manager*, which creates the appearance of a business trust or homeowner's association to be taxed, and treated in court as a corporation.

North American Realty Services Inc. (NARS) Facilitator and Consultant

Established in 1984, the company now known as NARS began as a provider of continuing real estate education to licensed Realtors® relative to various types of joint-ownership and land trust transfer transactions (equity sharing and shared appreciation mortgages). *See, e.g., IRC §280A.*

Through its legal resources and its close association with the trustee entities with whom NARS now works, final development of the Equity Holding "NEHTrust™" was completed in the latter part of 1992 as the result of the combined efforts of the author and attorney, Martin R. Slater, of PAC Holdings Corporation and the law firm of *Johnson, Poulsen, Coons and Slater,* Los Angeles, CA.

As of this writing, NARS has served in excess of 10,000 satisfied joint-ownership clients, including nearly 5,000 NEHTrust™ clients and many more thousands of Realtors® and real estate investors.

NOTE: When a NEHTrust™ transaction is overseen by North American Realty Services, Inc. and reviewed and approved by its legal advisors, NARS assumes full responsibility for its part in preparation and construction of the transaction and its related and expertly prepared attendant documentation. It is important to note that as of this writing, no past clients, affiliates, or certified NARS Professional Network members have ever been implicated in legal disputes concerning the structure, functionality, practicality, legality or enforceability of any aspect of the NEHTrust™ concept. It might also be noted that neither has there been a failure in, or impediment to, eviction of an errant resident co-beneficiary because of default or nonperformance.

When you hear of something that sounds "too good to be true," check it out. There's a good chance that it's both: that's what millionaires do, and why some are really millionaires.

Bill Gatten

A Fortune in Free Real Estate

EIGHT

SOME OF THE MOST
FREQUENTLY ASKED QUESTIONS

Q: Can a NEHTrust™ resident co-beneficiary (as tenant and assignee of beneficiary interest) legally vacate the trust property before the end of the agreement?

A: Yes. With the approval of the other beneficiary/ies a resident beneficiary may lease or rent the property out, sell their interest, or even leave the property vacant, so long as the respective financial interests of the other parties are not compromised. And permission for the resident beneficiary to do any of these things may not be unreasonably withheld.

Q: Can a NEHTrust™ CO-BENEFICIARY UNILATERALLY (ACTING ALONE) TERMINATE THE NEHTRUST™ BEFORE THE END OF THE AGREEMENT?

A: No. Once the NEHTrust™ transaction has been established between parties, only a breach of contract by a co-beneficiary would allow another beneficiary (settlor, investor or resident) to act alone on any issue relative to the parties, the transaction, the trust or the trust property.

Q: CAN THE NEHTRUST™ BE USED IN BUYING OR SELLING COMMERCIAL PROPERTY?

A: Yes. A land trust can hold commercial property. As a matter-of-fact, multiple beneficiaries can hold varying percentages of beneficial interest in such a trust. Do note, however, that specific protections under the "Garn-St. Germain Act" (i.e., allowing transfer of 1 to 4 units to a revocable, inter vivos trust) extend only to residential property (of fewer than five units.)...and not to commercial property of five units or more. Therefore, a lender's express permission to vest commercial property, or five or more residential units in a land trust should be obtained from the lender prior to doing so.

Q: WHAT HAPPENS IF A BENEFICIARY DIES DURING THE TERM OF A NEHTRUST™?

A. Upon death of a beneficiary, its interests and obligations in the land trust and related documentation pass to the heirs (thereby avoiding probate). The heirs then assume precisely the same obligations, responsibilities, rights and benefits that the original beneficiary held. Nothing changes.

If it were to be a *resident* or *investor* beneficiary who died, and the heirs were to fail to honor the obligations of the agreement, eviction would follow. The beneficiary interests of the defaulting parties would then be extinguished by the methods prescribed in the original documentation.

Q: HOW WOULD ONE WHO PLACED A HOME INTO A NEHTRUST™, VERSUS SELLING IT OUTRIGHT, BE VIEWED RELATIVE TO AN APPLICATION FOR A NEW HOME LOAN (RE. THE STANDARD *DEBT-TO-INCOME RATIO* PENALTY)?

A: By having relinquishing the property to a two or three beneficiary NEHTrust™ arrangement, the former title holder (the settlor beneficiary) should be seen by a prospective mortgage lender as having effectively disposed of the property on a *Contingent Sale* basis (i.e., as if it had been sold via a Wrap-Around, Contract for Deed or Lease-Purchase arrangement). This then means that the standard expenses of managing income property have, for all practical purposes, been eliminated. There should, therefore, be no income-to-debt penalty imposed for potential management, maintenance and vacancy expenses.

The NEHTrust™ method of disposing of the property, coupled with the fact that the "tenant buyer (co-beneficiary)" is making higher payments than would be normal *fair market rent,* is virtually always considered sufficient to avoid the *debt-to-income-ratio* penalty. This is to say that rather than the new lender allowing only, say, 70% credit for their applicant's income from the relinquished property (as they would with a rental or lease of the property), they would—in light of there being no expenses—most likely allow 100% of such net income to be added to the borrowers other earned income (or not deducted from it) for purposes of determining the amount of the new loan.

Note that a standard form letter explaining the NEHTrust™ process can be submitted to one's prospective new mortgage lender, explaining the function and nuances of the transfer.

Q: WHAT HAPPENS WHEN (IF) A RESIDENT BENEFICIARY FAILS TO MAKE PAYMENTS WHEN DUE?

A: There are two separate consequences of a default by a resident beneficiary in a NEHTrust™:

a) Eviction, and

b) Extinguishment of the defaulting party's interest in the title-holding land trust:

1. **First Step—Termination of Occupancy:**

   By the terms of the NEHTrust's separate *lease agreement*, the party or entity acting as landlord (either the beneficiaries themselves, or a neutral entity appointed by them) has been instructed by all beneficiaries (the defaulting beneficiary included) to, in the event of payment default, issue a *Notice to Pay or Quit (generally a 3 or 5 day notice)*, followed, if necessary, by an *Unlawful Detainer Action.* The tenant in default is then removed from the property willingly or by court order with help from the local constabulary (police department, sheriff's department, constable's office, marshal's dept., etc.).

2. **Second Step—Termination of Beneficiary Interest in the Land Trust:**

   By the defaulting parties' own specific direction to the trustee (as per the original contract), a payment default by *any* tenant in the trust property who is also a beneficiary in the land trust, constitutes an offer by the defaulting beneficiary to sell all of its beneficiary interest to the non-defaulting party/ies at the property's *Fair Market Value at* the time of the eviction.

   It is further agreed in the original contract that such sale shall take place only after payment of a *Default Fee (of, say,* $2,000) and repayment of all past due amounts (missed payments, late charges, fees and penalties). *If* the defaulting party disagrees with the offer with which it is presented, it has thirty (30) days within which to challenge the offer by an MAI (*Member American Appraisal Institute*) appraisal in order to prove that more money is owed than was offered.

If it can be proven within the allotted time that the offer was inadequate, then the offer must be increased. However, note that the parties will already have agreed in the original documentation that any such *buy-out* of beneficiary interest is to be made in the form of an *unsecured promissory note*, which note is to become due and payable only upon the scheduled termination date of the trust, and only if the property sells for enough to cover such repayment following a return of all of the non-defaulting parties' respective contributions.

The design and purpose of this default remedy is to keep the *lease* and the *trust* separate from each other, and to allow for fair treatment and full recourse by the parties should either (any) of them be or feel maltreated by the other. This remedy is designed to be mutually punitive and protective.

Q: WHAT IF A NEHTRUST™ PROPERTY LOSES VALUE DURING THE TERM OF THE AGREEMENT?

A: Erosion of real estate values is, of course, always a possibility, and if, at the end of the term of the NEHTrust™, the property can't be sold (or purchased by the resident beneficiary) for enough to return the nonresident beneficiary's initial contribution (e.g., his/her beginning equity); and should the nonresident choose not to reduce the amount of its refundable contribution... then the resident beneficiary has these options:

1) Vacate the property with no further obligation, forfeiting its entire interest without refunds of any monies.

2) By mutual agreement, extend the contract.

3) Buy the property for the amount owed to the co-beneficiaries and retire or assume the underlying financing.

Note that, as is the case with any real estate purchase, down payment monies or costs of improvements can in fact be lost due to ordinary trends in real estate supply and demand.

One might also liken this risk scenario to a mortgage loan that is amortized over, say, thirty years, but that is due and payable in five years with a balloon payment (known as a "30-due-in-5"). If in such an arrangement, one is unable to meet his obligation at term, he/she has no choice but to either relinquish the property to the lender or sell it (if possible). The same is true of the Equity Holding Trust Transfer™ unless the parties mutually agree otherwise.

Q: HOW IS THE PROPERTY'S *"MUTUALLY AGREED VALUE (MAV)"* DETERMINED AT THE INCEPTION OF THE NEHTRUST™, SINCE THERE IS NO *SALE PRICE* PER SE?

A: The property's *MAV* is established and used purely for the purpose of determining a starting point for calculating the parties' respective refundable co-beneficiary contributions at the outset.

Such refundable contribution is analogous to the amount of "equity" one would have in the property when the transaction commences: i.e., the difference between the property's value and what is owed on it.

The property's true fair market value (FMV) is generally considered to be the *greater* of:

1) The property's true value as determined by an appraisal or inferred by a *Comparative Market Analysis;* or

2) An accepted "surcharge" value as may have been adjusted upward from the FMV in view of the acquiring party's lack of credit worthiness or limited cash; or

3) (When the settlor is to receive no refunds or profit share at termination) the amount of all existing loans and/or other encumbrances against the property.

Q: WHAT IS THE DIFFERENCE BETWEEN THE TERMS, "MUTUALLY AGREED VALUE (MAV)" AND "FAIR MARKET VALUE (FMV)" IN THE VERNACULAR OF THE EQUITY HOLDING TRUST™ TRANSFER (I.E., THE NEHTRUST™)?

A: *Fair Market Value* (FMV) is generally deemed to be a property's transfer value as would be agreed-to by a prudent buyer and a prudent seller. This amount is generally dictated by prevailing real estate market trends. The *Mutually Agreed Value* (MAV), on the other hand, is merely the sum of the existing encumbrances on the property, plus the amount of equity contribution that a seller or investor is leaving in the transaction (i.e., an amount to be repaid later). In other words, where a settlor beneficiary (the relinquishing party) in a NEHTrust™ leaves an existing $150,000 mortgage in place in exchange for receiving, say, $10,000 in cash five years later from a buyer, the *MAV* would be $160,000...even though the *Fair Market Value* might be much more than that amount.

Example #1:

The property's true FMV is $200,000

The existing mortgage balance is $170,000

The **Settlor Beneficiary** holds $30,000 in existing equity, but for his/her own reasons agrees to keep the loan in place for a buyer and take just $5,000 in cash up front with no further claims on the property, its income or future profits. He/She agrees to retain a cursory 10% beneficiary interest in the land trust (merely to avoid excessive taxation, insurance problems and due-on-sale violation), which beneficiary interest he/she agrees to forfeit to the investor beneficiary upon the trust's termination.

In this scenario the **Investor Beneficiary Contribution** now includes the $5,000 paid to Seller and, say, another $5,000 in closing costs ($10,000 total)...plus the remaining $25,000 in existing equity, and still another $5,000 in "bumped equity" (whereby an investor sets the MAV at an amount over and above the FMV as fair compensation for taking on a resident beneficiary with marginal credit and limited cash.

Now let's say the **Resident Beneficiary** comes in with $15,000 that is paid to the investor beneficiary at inception (constituting a 7.5% up-front cost).

Given all the foregoing parameters, the MAV for this transaction is $205,000: there being $25,000 owed to the investor at termination (i.e., $40,000, less the $15,000 received from the resident beneficiary). There is $15,000 to be refunded to the resident beneficiary for its original up-front cost.

Then at termination, after each party receives a return of its respective contribution, the remainder of any further net proceeds are shared among the beneficiaries with respect to each of their percentage of beneficiary interest in the trust (the investor, now being in possession of the forfeited 10% interest and profit potential that was held by the original settlor throughout the term of the agreement).

Example #2:

The property's true FMV - $180,000

The existing loan balance - $125,000

A resident beneficiary finds a seller who is willing to part with his/her property by just letting someone take over the existing loan without request for anything further.

In this example the MAV would be $125,000 while the FMV was $180,000.

In this same scenario, if the relinquishing party had opted to retain only, say, $15,000 of the existing equity to be paid at the trust's termination, the MAV would be set at $140,000.

Q: Could an acquiting party (resident or investor) benefit from the NEHTrust™ should the underlying loan on a property be greater than its value? (i.e., an over-encumbered property)?

A: Yes. The "over-encumbrance" on a NEHTrust™ property is often perceived as simply a *trade-off* for an acquiring party's inability to qualify for a standard mortgage loan, or its lack of a standard *down payment* and/or preferred credit. Because the NEHTrust™ purchase may avoid the mortgage approval traps of *self-employment, newness on the job, limited job history, or marginal (or no) credit history*—one planning on a long-term ownership might choose to disregard the property's over-encumbrance.

The fact is, that even if by the end of the agreement, the resale value of the property had not increased sufficiently to cover the loan against it, the resident will still have enjoyed the benefits of home ownership and income tax deductions that would have been unavailable otherwise...and at termination he/she still has the right to —

1) Petition to extend the agreement, or

2) Just move out and pay no more

Obviously, if the monthly (after-tax) payment were to be approximately the normal rent, and if the loan needn't be retired (paid-off) at any particular time soon, a NEHTrust™ buyer might find such an over-encumbrance completely inconsequential.

In other-words, at the NEHTrust's™ termination the resident beneficiary may not have made any money from appreciation: but neither did any of his/her friends and neighbors who purchased their homes traditionally at the same time.[44] And unlike those friends and neighbors, the NEHTrust™ resident beneficiary can freely walk away with no further obligations, while the others still have a burdensome property on their hands and 25 years of mortgage payments ahead of them.

Q: THE DUE-ON-SALE CLAUSE...COULD A MORTGAGE LENDER *CLAIM* THAT THE NEHTRUST™ VIOLATED ITS DUE-ON-SALE CLAUSE?

A: Though unlikely, the answer is yes. No one can predict what any commercial institution *could* *[might]* "claim" in the future...whether right or wrong.

However, beyond the borrower's transfer of the property to a trustee of his own inter vivos trust (fully authorized by federal legislation), none of the NEHTrust™ documents are, or need to be, recorded.: although, even if discovered by the lender, such documents involve only an appointment of a successor beneficiary and a lease of the property to that party, and neither of these actions are prohibited by law or any lender's due-on-sale clause.

Furthermore, since the NEHTrust™ transfer does not adversely impact the lender's security interest or ability to foreclose for cause, such a claim or assertion by a lender, even if brought, would likely be unenforceable.

Make no mistake about it, the Garn-St. Germain Act (12 U.S.C. 1701j-3) ("GSG"), a duly enacted federal law, provides that any borrower owning less than five units may, at its own discretion, place its property into a qualified living (inter vivos) trust at any time, so long as the borrower remains "a" beneficiary; so long as the trust is a revocable trust; and so long as the trust document does not transfer occupancy rights.

That same law (GSG) also allows the trust property to be leased out by means a subsequent and separate document, to whomever the borrower/settlor might choose to lease to (caveat: the lease may not be for *more than three years* and must not contain or relate to an *Option to Purchase* the property), irrespective of what a lender's "druthers" might otherwise be.

Nonetheless, even in view of the above, it is conceivable (though perhaps not probable) that a lender could one day declare the "intent" of the NARS NEHTrust™ to be contrary to their best interests, and assert that it somehow schemes to circumvent their ability to capitalize on their borrower's misfortune: i.e., an owner's inability to afford the payments any longer; its inability to dispose of the property without incurring a loss; the inability to lease without a major *negative cash flow*; or the inability to avoid major tax penalties relative to foreclosure and/or an *offer in compromise* (short sale).

If such a lender protest should ever occur, the court would first need to determine if any laws had been broken; as well as "how" and "*if*" the plaintiff had been injured. Therefore, in actuality, the true (real) effect of the NEHTrust™ is the protection of the lender's interests by the fact that it avoids:

1) alienation;

2) prohibited ownership transfer or title involvement; and

3) an unwise transfer of real property ownership under duress or threat of financial loss.

The *successor co-beneficiary* (the designated remainder entity) in a land trust does not receive *real estate* ownership, a bargain purchase price, a purchase option or a loan of monies. *If,* and/or *when,* such a co-beneficiary *would* choose to acquire title ownership of the property, the acquisition would be by means of an ordinary purchase offer to the beneficiaries or trustee followed by traditional mortgage qualifying and financing.

Q: MY RESEARCH SEEMS TO INDICATE THAT THERE'S A DISPARITY BETWEEN THE LAWS, I.E., BETWEEN TITLE 12 OF THE UNITED STATES CODE (12 U.S.C. 1701j-3) AND THE INTERPRETATION OF THAT LAW BY THE OFFICE OF THRIFT SUPERVISION IN THE CODE OF FEDERAL REGULATIONS (12 CFR 591). WHY IS THIS? AND WHICH ONE SHOULD I RELY ON?

A. 12 U.S.C. 1701j-3 and 12 CFR 591 do indeed differ in context. Understand, however, that the former is a federal law, enacted by Congress and signed by the President of the United States (FDIRA 1982), which specifically allows for the transfer of a lender's security (the mortgaged property) by a borrower into an inter vivos trust, when the borrower is, and remains, *"A"* beneficiary therein (i.e., 'one of more than one').

The U.S. Code also clearly and specifically declares that, absent a reasonable clause to the contrary in a loan document, a borrower remains wholly free and welcome to let (lease-out) the mortgaged property anytime he/she would elect to do so (i.e., assuming a 3-year maximum lease term, and assuming that the lease would not involve or relate to a contractual option to purchase).

On the other hand, included in the *Code of Federal Regulations* (the CFR, a compilation of the promulgations of the various governmental regulatory bodies) is an interpretation this issue by the Office of Thrift Supervision of the law, which is contradictory. It infers that a borrower who would create an inter vivos trust (to hold a mortgaged property of 4 or fewer units), must be **"THE"** (i.e., the *only*) beneficiary of such a trust; and that the trust property itself can never be vacated (much less rented or leased out).

One would think that such a prohibition against renting, were it to be supported by the courts, would put a pretty hefty crimp in the practices of those borrowers who hold duplexes, triplexes and *four-plexes* in inter vivos trusts. It is strongly believed by this author (though there can obviously be no guaranty) that any such claim by a lender insisting upon the CFR's inaccurate misconstruction of a federal code section would be summarily struck down should it be presented as support for a claim of alienation.

Q: IN THEIR 100+ YEARS OF USE IN THE U.S., HAVE LAND TRUSTS EVER BEEN CHALLENGED BY LENDERS WHO CLAIMED HAVING BEEN DAMAGED BY AN UNRECORDED AND PRIVATE ASSIGNMENT OF A LAND TRUST'S BENEFICIAL INTEREST TO A THIRD PARTY?

A: Yes. However, one must bear in mind that the land trust in *most* states (e.g., all but nine) is not a "statutory" device. This essentially means that there is no statute (legislated law) addressing it (yet) and that its existence is allowed and governed by a *fiction of law:* rules of Equity or court-decided legal precedents established within related court cases.

In most states the land trust is wholly acceptable (even if not fully authorized) by virtue of its exclusion from specific prohibitions under a jurisdiction's "Statute of Land Uses," acceptance of the "Doctrine of Equitable Conversion," and/ or by virtue of a state's trust law relative to inter vivos trusts in general.

Although we know of no cases in recent years (attempts by lenders to foreclose for reasons of land trust beneficiary interest assignments), a few such actions have been brought in the past (mostly in Illinois)—and in every case wherein the borrower was a natural person, the decision of the court was invariably in favor of the defendant (the borrower...i.e., the lenders lost). [45]

Q: SINCE NARS HAS ITS OWN ATTORNEYS AND ACCOUNTANTS, SHOULD I CONSULT WITH MY OWN LEGAL AND ACCOUNTING ADVISORS REGARDING THE FEASIBILITY OF THE NEHTRUST™ IN MY STATE AND FOR MY SITUATION?

A: Yes, certainly. One should always seek out and heed the advice of his/her own competent legal and tax advisors, as well as seeking one's own independent real estate agency advice.

The problem that exists, however, is that very few attorneys (even real estate specialists) are at all familiar with the nature of the land trust, and what makes it so different from all other trust forms (i.e., it's being beneficiary directed, the property's equitable title being vested in the trustee, immunity from partition and charging orders; its conversion of ownership of realty to that of personalty, etc.).

NARS welcomes inquiries from all legal and accounting professionals and/or their clients, however, its legal staff may actively represent only the best interests of NARS and its affiliates, and not necessarily those of clients or inquiring parties.

Q: ARE MOST ATTORNEYS AND ACCOUNTANTS FAMILIAR WITH THE NEHTRUST™ OR THE WORKINGS OF THE "TITLE-HOLDING LAND TRUST" (I.E., THE UNDERPINNING OF THE NEHTRUST™) IN GENERAL?

A: No (not by any means). As a matter-of-fact, as stated above, in most states where there is no specific land trust legislation, were one to interview 100 attorneys, perhaps twenty-five *might* be familiar with, or even accustomed to working with, trusts in general. Then of those twenty-five, it is unlikely that you'd find even one who is well acquainted with the specifics and subtleties of "title-holding" land trusts.

The best advice is to ask the attorney's specific knowledge of the intricacies of the *"Illinois Land Trust,"* which is the model for the NEHTrust™ in all states. If the attorney advises against the use of the land trust and deigns to suggest another device in its place, make sure you get an affirmative answer to *all of* the following questions concerning the benefits of the NEHTRUST™ .

With all due respect, does your suggested alternative...

1. Avoid violating the lender's due on sale clause rather than just sneaking around it?

2. Protect the property from either (any) parties' legal problems (lawsuits, creditor judgments, IRS liens; marital dissolution, bankruptcy and probate?

3. Allow for simple eviction of, versus foreclosure upon, a defaulting tenant/buyer?

4. Avoid the possibility of a defaulting party's claim of having an *equitable interest* in the property, in order to thwart eviction and to force lengthy and costly judicial processes?

5. Avoid the necessity for payment of capital gains taxes until the termination of the agreement?

6. Allow for the transfer of income tax benefits to a tenant/buyer without a title

transfer or a transfer of equitable interest in the property, thereby multiplying net income?

7. Allow for continuous occupancy beyond three years without an equitable conveyance or a due-on-sale violation (re. 12 USC1701j-3)?

8. Provide watertight title protection by means of a continuous "escrow" process wherein no party can act with regard to the property without the express consent and direction of all the parties.

9. Protect all parties from one party's changing its mind in favor of making a "sweeter deal" for him/herself (i.e., backing out of a lease option or CFD when the stakes get higher)?

10. Avoid transfer and conveyance tax and/or stamps upon full transfer of home ownership benefits?

11. Avoid reassessment for property tax upon sale or transfer?

Choosing your professional advisor based upon the fact that he/she is knowledgeable in real estate matters, the fact that he or she is a "great attorney," or the fact that he/she is a "super accountant," or even a "trusted friend," will not serve your needs with respect to your use of the NEHTRUST™.

A qualified and objective professional evaluation of all aspects of the NEHTrust™ transfer as pertinent to current real estate law, trust law, probate law and state and federal income tax law is crucial.

Q: CAN NARS RECOMMEND A GOOD ATTORNEY WHO IS FAMILIAR WITH LAND TRUSTS?

A: In some, but not all states, the answer is "Yes." However any truly conscientious and *honest* attorney can and will always do one of the following three things when presented with the NEHTrust™ concept for the first time. And if they don't, find another attorney...fast:

1) Do all the research and review necessary to make a wise recommendation to his her client (lots of hours), or...

2) Analyze the components of the NEHTrust™ separately: not as a trust within itself, but rather as a system that merely utilizes a revocable living trust at its core along with a lease agreement. In other words, if the lease agreement is acceptable, and the appointment of a remainder or successor manger-beneficiary by assignment is acceptable, the only questions remaining to validate the NEHTrust™ should be:

• Are inter vivos trusts legal in this state? Are express inter vivos trusts allowed? That is, might a nominee or grantor trust be created and utilized for any legitimate purpose?

• Does this state recognize the *Doctrine of Equitable Conversion?* In other words, is the merger of legal title and equitable title allowed? We know that such merger is allowed in all states except for Louisiana and Tennessee: In Louisiana the beneficiary interest in a land trust would be

85

characterized as a "right" encumbering the property," rather than ownership of either realty or personalty; whereas in Tennessee the state fails to separate personalty from realty in trusts of any type.

• What powers must a trustee have to avoid characterization as a dry, passive or failed trust?

• Are there any court cases that would specifically deny or negate the practical application of Illinois-type land trusts in this state?

• Does this attorney understand clearly that the NEHTrust is comprised of four transactions and not just one:

   i   *the land trust;*

   ii   *the appointment of a successor beneficiary;*

   iii   *the agreement between parties re. future profits; and then*

   iv   *the leasing of the property by one of the beneficiaries?*

3. Refer you to another attorney who is more qualified to render an honest recommendation, versus what most do: arbitrarily, and solely for the sake of time and the hourly charge, suggest some inferior form of seller-assisted, subject-to financing (options, land contracts, equity shares, wraps, etc.) that you are trying so desperately to avoid and protect yourself from.

Q: WHAT WOULD HAPPEN IN THE EVENT OF AN IRRECONCILABLE DISPUTE BETWEEN CO-BENEFICIARIES IN A NEHTRUST™?

A: Although such occurrences are rare due to the *third-party ownership* aspect of the NEHTrust™, disputes between parties can and do arise from time to time, but seldom if ever do they impede the original objectives of the arrangement.

Holding property under the ownership of a land trust trustee can be thought of as similar to holding a property in third-party escrow by a settlement agent. Doing so prevents misdealing and untoward actions by any party against another during the settlement process.

Nonetheless, NEHTrust™ beneficiaries do contractually agree in advance, that if irreconcilable differences do arise, they are to be settled by arbitration under the rules of the *American Arbitration Association.* Each party agrees that it will abide by, and rely upon, the decision of the appointed arbitrator. Do note, however, that we have never known of a single NEHTrust™ to go to arbitration, or even of any irreconcilable dispute having occurred. All terms and conditions are hammered out in advance and must be strictly adhered to, and the requirement for unanimous direction seems to have very adequately quelled any disagreements among beneficiaries.

Q: WHAT WOULD STOP A SETTLOR, IN HIS OWN *REVOCABLE TRUST* (A TRUST WHICH IS SET UP IN HIS/ HER OWN NAME AND REVOCABLE BY HIM/HER), FROM REVOKING IT TO THE DETRIMENT OF THE OTHER BENEFICIARY/IES?

A: Of prime importance is the fact that, even though the trust that underpins the NEHTrust™ is a revocable trust, it is directed by ALL of its beneficiaries mutually (i.e., the *Power of Direction* is unanimous). In other words, unless special provisions were to have been made in advance, no single beneficiary or group of beneficiaries can direct the property's legal owner (the trustee) to do anything, sign anything or approve anything involving the property or its title, without the absolute concurrence and mutual direction of all the beneficiaries.

Since the trustee must be involved in any action concerning the trust and its corpus, a beneficiary acting unilaterally (alone) can not alter the trust agreement, borrow money on the property, or bring about a lien against it...without the full agreement, acceptance and direction of the other beneficiary/ies. For example, a resident beneficiary wanting to add a room, install a swimming pool, or encumber the property, may not do so without the knowledge, consent, and mutual direction of the other beneficiaries.

Q: AS A PROSPECTIVE SELLER, OR BUYER, INTERESTED IN THE NEHTRUST™, HOW AND WHERE DO I BEGIN?

A: You may contact NARS by phone (1-800-20-SHARE) or on the Web at *www.landtrust.net* or contact the investor, seller, buyer or real estate professional who provided you with this book.

Be assured that irrespective of how you choose to proceed from this point, NARS and its legal, accounting and documentation experts will be happy to work closely with you throughout your transaction, from inception to termination.

Upon request, and for a fee, NARS will handle all client conferencing and consultation; prepare all relevant documentation; provide, and interface with, the selected corporate trustee, escrow and the third-party collection service. NARS will work hand-in-hand with your buyers, sellers, investors, Realtors®, lender(s), and/or the designated closing attorneys, escrow officers and/or title companies that you select.

Q: **WHAT ARE THE STANDARD COSTS FOR ESTABLISHING A THE NEHTRUST™?**

A: Apart from any Realtors® commissions, settlement fees, appraisals, contingency funds, etc., typical Closing Costs for a NEHTrust™ transaction (including both the *seller's and acquiring party's* costs) vary from 0.375% to 1.0% *(3/8ths of a percent to one percent)* of a residential property's mutually agreed value (MAV) at inception. The trustee acceptance fee and the NARS consulting fee (including facilitation and documentation) generally comprise no more than 1/4th to 1/3rd (or less) of all settlement/closing costs.

Do note that other costs (beyond and above the NARS consulting, acceptance and setup fees) could include, but be not limited to:

• The escrow (closing agent's) fee;

• Title insurance;

• Prorated and advance property taxes;

• Initial hazard insurance premium;

• Initial home warranty insurance premiums;

• Initial mortgage insurance premium;

- Credit report;

- Pest inspection;

- Mandatory geological survey (soil) reports;

- Back payments, taxes and insurance;

- Preparation/filing of Notice of Fiduciary Responsibility (IRS Form 56-A)

Although not a part of the "closing costs" per se, one should take care, as well, to budget at closing for the first monthly payment that will be due on the contract; and for at least one or two aggregate monthly payments to be held in the contingency fund (as a buffer for delayed payments, unexpected repairs, etc.).

Q: **Is there a minimum or maximum allowable term for a NEHTrust™?**

A: Yes. Relative to a *maximum length* of term, a land trust would be deemed invalid if, creditors were unable to reach the property for an indefinite period of time. The trust must contain a stipulated termination date (...and carry a "Perpetuities Savings Clause" relative to the *Rule Against Perpetuities*).

Regarding the Rule Against Perpetuities[46] (applied to avoid perpetual trusteeship and the unending shielding of an asset from creditor claimants), disallowed are:

1) land trusts with terms exceeding twenty-one years,

2) Land trusts without a precisely stated shorter term, or...

3) Land trusts in which any *remainder interests* exceeds the stated term of the Agreement (as regards successor beneficiaries or successor trustees)

The maximum trust term is twenty-one years; however, with proper contract verbiage, the land trust that is the underpinning for the NEHTrust™ may extend for the term of the property's underlying mortgage financing, if greater than twenty-one years without compromising the *Rule Against Perpetuities.*

As far as *minimum* term requirements, there really are none; however we do recommend a two-year minimum limit in most cases. The reason for this is that if the trust's term were to conflict with certain tax deferment or exemption provisions, a short trust term may not serve the holding requirements for **IRC** §1031 like-kind tax-deferred exchange of investment real estate.

If, however, one is not planning to reside in the property, and a future *IRC §1031 like-kind tax deferred exchange* is not contemplated, then a minimum holding requirement is a moot point.

A Fortune in Free Real Estate

Give me a home where the buffalo roam, and where seldom is heard a discouraging word, and I'll show you a bargain fixer-upper.

Bill Gatten

A Fortune in Free Real Estate

NINE

RELATIVE RISK AND COST ANALYSIS

The chart that follows is designed to graphically demonstrate the relative cost and degree of risk (danger) entailed in virtually *any* method of disposing of one's real estate by other than traditional means. For all practical purposes, if an outright sale (with full credit qualification, down-payment and standard "finding" period) is not feasible or possible, then one's options truly are limited to those shown in the accompanying *Benefits to Risk Chart.*

When reviewing the chart, take care to note that aside from the options shown, there are no other alternatives for a distressed seller with an unwanted property, other than staying in the property and continuing to make payments on it...or continuing to try to sell it via the conventional method.

Please note that when calculating potential costs for options "A" and "B" on the chart (re. the *offer-in-compromise or foreclosure*), any expenses incurred by the lender that will be attributed as *debt-relief* to the seller (the owner in default) can be exorbitant and likely will include:

- Debt relief (the taxable difference between the amount owed to the lender and the ultimate amount received by the lender upon sale)

- Real Estate commissions paid-out by the lender

- Administrative expenses directly attributable to the compromise or foreclosure

- Unpaid principal relative to any missed (unmade) payments

- Unpaid property taxes and/or insurance costs incurred by the lender

- Maintenance, refurbishment, repair, upkeep and costs incurred by the lender in maintaining the property and readying it for resale

Note: Many unwary homeowners who undertake to ease their *Pain* by means of sacrificing their credit (and too often, their self-esteem) via an *Offer and Compromise,* or by just walking away from their loan responsibilities ("letting the bank take it back"), are stunned when they receive their IRS Form 1099 from the lender, requiring that income tax be paid on their "windfall" debt relief, as if such mortgage relief had been money paid to them.

The income tax due on *Debt-Relief* can be, and most often will be, thousands upon thousands of dollars more than what the total costs of allowing someone else to take over the property and the mortgage payments by means of a NARS Equity Holding Trust™ might have been.

For the Real Estate Investor: Uncover a distressed property owner's "Pain" and offer a quick and safe cure. As reflected in the following pages, there are few, if any, options beyond the Equity Holding Trust™ that are safer, less costly, less damaging to the seller, or more logical. In other words, the property owner need but vest the property with a land trust trustee, make you a beneficiary and lease it to you or your assignee for the full payment amount, plus all costs of maintenance, repairs, management, insurance and property taxes.

For the Realtor®: By way of a thorough understanding and use of the Equity Holding Trust™ concept, you are one of the very few in your field that can offer a distressed seller a viable solution and a "way out" that will not damage his/her credit or bank account, or bring about exorbitant costs, tax penalties and inconvenience.

For the seller: If you are contemplating any form of seller-assisted financing, do carefully consider the use of the Equity Holding Trust™ as a means to avoid all the cost, time, aggravation and myriad risks of dealing with an unwanted or burdensome property. In other words, let someone else with different needs and a different agenda take over the property, the loan, the responsibility and your discontent. After all: *Isn't one man's trash another man's treasure?*

For the buyer: For anyone seeking a new home—but especially for the cash, credit and/or income challenged—the NARS Equity Holding Trust™ can provide a marvelous means for obtaining the *benefits of homeownership* without the standard down-payment and credit requirements, and without the extreme risks and worry that are so much a part of the many surreptitious "creative financing schemes" in vogue today.

Interestingly, for buyers, sellers, agents and investors alike, even over-encumbered properties can often present great opportunities for buyers and distressed sellers alike through use of the NEHTrust™. For example, note that the assumption of any aged loan, even though at an amount greater than the property's value, can actually be no more (or even less) expensive than obtaining a new, lower interest rate loan for a lesser amount. Compare the following two scenarios to see if one is any better than the other:

1. $200,000 home requiring a 10% down payment, stringent credit requirements, and a 30-year $180,000 mortgage with payments of $1,300 per month.

    $20,000 down+$3,000 closing costs + payment stream of **$491,000** including up-front costs.

2. An identical $200,000 home that can be obtained *without* a down payment or bank qualifying, but which secures a seven year-old $210,000 loan balance, with monthly payments of $1,455 for 23 more years.

    $2,000 closing costs + payment stream of **$403,000** including up-front costs

One last comment regarding use of the *Benefits to Risk Chart* that follows:

Understand that when using this chart for analyzing ones options for disposition of an unwanted property by other than conventional means, the form serves two primary functions:

1. To allow for a comparison of the many unnecessary risks inherent in creative real estate financing in general; and

2. To allow a prospective seller to clearly see what the respective costs would likely be with any seller-assisted financing arrangement (as compared to the risks and costs of the NARS Equity Holding Trust™ Transfer.

From this standpoint, it should be clear that a qualified Realtor® or real estate investor would be quite justified in expecting most sellers toassist in financing the cost of the transaction and/or share in the cost of onerous continuing monthly payments (e.g., payment obligations that are in excess of fair market rent, which would necessitate a negative cash flow for an investor). Say, for instance, a seller was faced with needing to pay $20,000 in income tax on debt-relief relative to an offer and compromise on an over-encumbered property...won't he fare much better by paying, say, $5,000-$10,000 to the party relieving his burden by taking the property and the payments over? And/or might that person also agree to continue paying part of the continuing monthly payment obligation (after all, $250 per-month paid to the problem solver for, say, 36 months is less than half of the $20,000 that would otherwise be owed to the IRS)?

Or ...consider the example of a seller faced with a below-market offer along with the costs of closing, real estate commissions and income tax due on a previous capital gain (e.g., old 2nd mortgage). Might that person be willing to pay someone to relieve his "Pain" (as it were)?

A Fortune in Free Real Estate

In any selling situation, every statement made must be succinct ... and followed by absolute silence until the other person speaks.

Bill Gatten

A Fortune in Free Real Estate

The Benefit to Risk Chart

The chart that follows is a quick reference guide for determining one's best course of action relative to various alternatives to the traditional sale. With it, one can quickly determine the safest and least costly alternative available.

Note carefully, the many hidden dangers *(legal "time bombs")* lurking within the structure of virtually every "creative financing scheme" available. The protective shielding provided by the NARS Equity Holding Trust™ will, in most cases (if not all), far more than justify its use in terms of safety, cost savings and asset protection.

One should consider the NARS Equity Holding Trust™ Transfer as *the way* to accomplish the objectives of these "other" financing devices, not as an *alternative* to them.

COMMON COST AND BENEFIT-TO-RISK CHART

T R A N S A C T I O N	1. RISK OF DESTRUCTION OF THE SELLER'S CREDIT STANDING FOR YEARS TO COME — ASIDE FROM BANKRUPTCY, HOME FORECLOSURE OR A LENDERS FORCED OFFER AND COMPROMISE ARE AMONG THE WORST DAMAGE TO ONE'S CREDIT	2. RISK OF ONEROUS TAXATION ON DEBT RELIEF — UNLESS INSOLVENT BEFORE SELLING, ALL RESULTING DEBT-RELIEF WILL LIKELY RESULT IN SIGNIFICANT FEDERAL AND STATE INCOME TAXATION	3. RISK OF TRIGGERING THE LENDER'S DUE-ON-SALE CLAUSE — RE. UNDERLYING FINANCING (ESPECIALLY IN FNMA, GNMA, FHA, AND VA, LOANS)	4. RISK OF JEOPARDY TO TITLE AND SALABILITY OF THE PROPERTY: TO THE POINT OF IMPEDING OR ELIMINATING THE RIGHT TO SELL OR REFINANCE	5. RISK OF EITHER PARTY'S LIENS, SUITS, JUDGMENTS, BK, TAX LIENS OR MARITAL DISPUTES — ANY OF THESE CAN SERIOUSLY AFFECT TITLE THE PROPERTY'S, TITLE THUS... NEGATIVELY IMPACTING ON THE OTHER PARTY
A: SHORT-SALE	Probable Risk	Definite Risk	Little if Any Risk	Little if Any Risk	Little if Any Risk
B: FORECLOSURE	Definite Risk	Definite Risk	Little if Any Risk	Little if Any Risk	Little if Any Risk
C: RENTAL/LEASE	Little if Any Risk	Little if Any Risk	Little if Any Risk	Little if Any Risk	Little if Any Risk
D: LEASE OPTION	Little if Any Risk	Little if Any Risk	Minimal Risk	Minimal Risk	Probable Risk
E: LEASE–PURCHASE	Little if Any Risk	Little if Any Risk	Probable Risk	Definite Risk	Definite Risk
F: WRAP-AROUND	Little if Any Risk	Little if Any Risk	Probable Risk	Definite Risk	Definite Risk
G: CONTRACT FOR DEED	Little if Any Risk	Little if Any Risk	Probable Risk	Definite Risk	Definite Risk
H: EQUITY SHARE	Little if Any Risk	Little if Any Risk	Minimal Risk	Definite Risk	Probable Risk
I: EQ. HOLDING TRUST™	Little if Any Risk	Little if Any Risk	Little if Any Risk	Little if Any Risk	Little if Any Risk

RISK EVALUATION ---

Definite Risk 🔥🔥🔥🔥 (4 bombs)
Probable Risk 🔥🔥🔥 (3 bombs)
Minimal Risk 🔥🔥 (2 bombs)
Little if Any Risk (single icon)

RE. ALL FORMS OF SELLER-CARRY FINANCING

CHANCE OF EVICTION BECOMING IMPOSSIBLE — FORECLOSURE ACTION MAY BECOME NECESSARY TO REMOVE AN ERRANT TENANT... AN OPTIONOR COULD EVEN HAVE TO REFUND OPTION FEES, IMPROVEMENTS ... OR RENTS	THE COURT'S ABILITY TO *PARTITION* "*REAL PROPERTY*" *(REALTY)* CAN ALLOW LIENS AGAINST THE PROPERTY, AND CAN FORCE SALE: EVEN WHEN/IF OWNERSHIP IS "*UNDIVIDED*" AND HELD AS *TENANTS IN COMMON*	CHANCE OF UNTOWARD OR ACCIDENTAL ACTS OF THE OTHER PARTY — ONE MUST ALWAYS BE CONCERNED WITH REGARD TO THE PROPERTY AND ITS TITLE (E.G., JR. LOANS OR LIENS, CREDITOR LIENS, TAX LIENS, SUITS, BK.'S, ETC.).	CHANCE OF DEALING WITH A DISHONEST SELLER — A BUYER'S DESIRE WILL LIKELY BE DIMINISHED, IN THAT A DISHONEST PERSON CAN EASILY SELL, ENCUMBER, OR EVEN RE-*LEASE* THE PROPERTY WITHOUT THE RESIDENT'S CONSENT OR KNOWLEDGE	HIGH [MONTHLY] COST POTENTIAL FOR RE. MGT, MTCE, REPAIRS, NEGATIVE CASH-FLOW AND VACANCIES	ESTIMATE ALL COSTS (E.G., CLOSING COSTS, FEES, COMMIS., RFRBSMT, BRINGING THE PMTS, INS, TAXES, CURRENT ETC.,	MONTHLY INCOME/LOSS FROM THE PROPERTY AFTER THE TRANSACT'N (E.G., 0.6% TO 0.7% - 1.0% X PROP VALUE P/MO. IS STANDARD FOR RENT IN MOST AREAS)	CALCULATE TOTAL POSITIVE OR NEGATIVE CASH-FLOW PER-MONTH OVER NEXT 24 MONTHS	TOTAL COST
6.	**7.**	**8.**	**9.**	**10.**	**11.**	**12.**	**13.**	**14.**
--	--	--	--	--	$	$	$	$	
(icon)	(icon)	(icon)	(icon)	(icon)	$	$	$	$	
(icon)	(icon)	(icon)	(icon)	(icon)	$	$	$	$	
(icons)	(icons)	(icon)	(icon)	(icons)	$	$	$	$	
(icons)	(icons)	(icons)	(icon)	(icons)	$	$	$	$	
(icons)	(icons)	(icons)	(icon)	(icons)	$	$	$	$	
(icons)	(icons)	(icons)	(icon)	(icon)	$	$	$	$	
(icons)	(icons)	(icons)	(icon)	(icon)	$	$	$	$	
(icon)	(icon)	(icon)		(icon)	$	$	$	$	

BEST OPTION RELATIVE TO COST _____

BEST OPTION RELATIVE TO RISK _____

BEST OPTION RELATIVE TO BENEFIT _____

A Fortune in Free Real Estate

TEN

RENTAL PROPERTY INCOME LAYERING

Think about it: when a *gentleman rancher* (the rich guy who just wants to get away from the city) butchers a pig, it is cut up and nicely wrapped in packages of pork chops, pork loins, hams, spare ribs, and bacon. And the leftovers are loaded into a dumpster and hauled away, leaving the rancher with little chance of any real profit, considering the costs of the care and feeding of his stock.

However when a *real* pig farmer (the guy with slop on his boots, who depends on the farm for his living) butchers a pig, it a different story. The real (professional) pig farmer, after the butchering, ends up with all of the same extra pig-parts, with which he makes big profits in addition to just selling pork. He sells the pig skin for footballs; pig hair for paint brushes; pig ears for dog toys; pig snouts for...(hot dog filler?); pigs hooves for gelatin and/or pickled pig's feet; pig tails for (...something, I'm sure). Even the porcine intestinal mucosal lining of the porker is sold to the pharmaceutical industry for production of the lifesaving anticoagulant, Heparin. And anything left over is sold to producers of bone meal or dog food.

With this analogy in mind, doesn't it stand to reason that *landlords* might profit by taking the lead of the pig farmer, i.e., to stop being satisfied with just the gentlemanly sale of a rental property's *Use* and *Occupancy*, when so many other saleable components are available as well?

107

The charts on the following pages were designed to graphically demonstrate:

1) How an income-property owner can increase (even *double and triple*) his/her hard fought net rental income; while simultaneously reducing the cost of *use* and *occupancy* for the tenant in the same property...in the same process. Interestingly, the vast majority of "landlords," simply fail to realize that negative cash-flow; maintenance and repair costs; and all other residential income property expenses and burdens can be eliminated virtually overnight by merely collecting more money from the tenant, in exchange for something of even *greater* value.

2) How most rental tenants and lessees could cut their rental costs in half (or even live rent-free over time), if they could just gain access to all, or *some*, of their landlord's *mortgage interest, income tax deductions, loan principal reduction, equity buildup,* and *appreciation* potential.

   a) The transaction illustrated on the following page is a 50:50 Equity Holding Trust™ equity share, wherein the tenant has been given a 50% beneficiary interest in the Equity Holding Trust™ and, therefore, a 50% share in future profits.

   b) The property's hypothetical fair market value (FMV) at inception is $150,000, with a $140,000 loan against it.

   c) The owner (landlord) has $10,000 in equity at inception.

d) The Fair Market Rent from inception is 0.653% of the property's Fair Market Value.

e) Appreciation shown is calculated at a modest 3% per-year of the FMV at inception.

f) The monthly maintenance and repair costs for the property are shown at a normal average of 1% percent per-year.

g) The monthly vacancy factor is calculated at the normal two rental payments per-year wherein no rental income is forthcoming, but payments must nonetheless be made to the lender (in addition to management, maintenance, advertising/marketing and showing costs).

h) The presumption here is that the average reduction in the mortgage principal is $100 per-month (i.e., $3,600 over 36 months).

SALABLE LAYERS

RESIDENTIAL PROPERTY PROFIT CENTERS

Property's Value =	$ 150,000
Encumbrance(s) =	$ 140,000
Existing Equity =	$ 10,000
P/I + Tax & Ins =	$ 1,310
Reg. Rental Income =	**$ 980**

Example Based Upon a 3 yr NEHTrust™

$ 980.00	◀	Use/Occupancy (Rent) ▶	$ 980.00
$ 138.00	◀	50% of Existing Equity ▶	$ 102.48
		50% of Principal Reduction	
$ 50.00	◀	(mortgage pay-down) ▶	$ 27.55
$ 490.00	◀	Income Tax Deductions ▶	$ 270.25
		(e.g. assuming 1/3rd tax bracket)	
$ 193.18	◀	50% of Appreciation Potential ▶	$ 106.54
		(Say, 3% per year for 3 years)	
$?	◀	Mineral Rights / Appurtenances ▶	$?
		Pride of Ownership/Quiet Enjoyment	
		(In exchange for mgmt. and mtce.)	

New Monthly Rental Income	$1,486.82
New Pos. Cash-Flow	$ 183.00
Elimination of Vacancy & Mtce.	$ 288.00

NET INCREASE IN RENTAL INCOME: $794.82

Mo. Mtce Cost Eliminated (e.g., 1%/yr) :   **$125.00**

Mo. Vacancies Eliminated (e.g., 2 pmts/yr) : **$163.00**

Note that in the above scenario, considering even a 3% per-year average annual appreciation rate, the tenant's rental expense is offset by $316.84 per-month over 3 years for a total of $11,406.00. Note that even if there had been no appreciation over that time, the offset would still constitute a tenant savings of $124.00 per-month or $4,500 over the same 3 years.

SALABLE LAYERS

RESIDENTIAL PROPERTY PROFIT CENTERS

Property's Value = $ _____
Encumbrance(s) = $ _____
Existing Equity = $ _____
P/I + Tax & Ins = $ _____
Reg. Rental Income = $ _____

Example Based Upon a 3 yr NEHTrust™

$_____	Use/Occupancy (Rent)	$_____
$_____	50% of Existing Equity	$_____
	50% of Principal Reduction	
$_____	(mortgage pay-down)	$_____
$_____	Income Tax Deductions	$_____
	(e.g. assuming 1/3rd tax bracket)	
$_____	50% of Appreciation Potential	$_____
	(Say, 3% per year for 3 years)	
$_____	Mineral Rights / Appurtenances	$_____
	Pride of Ownership/Quiet Enjoyment	
	(In exchange for mgmt. and mtce.)	

New Monthly Rental Income $_____
New Pos. Cash-Flow $_____
Elimination of Vacancy & Mtce. $_____

NET INCREASE IN RENTAL INCOME -$_____

Mo. Mtce Cost Eliminated (e.g., 1%/yr) - $_____

Mo. Vacancies Eliminated (e.g., 2 pmts/yr) -$_____

This blank chart is for use in calculating the amounts of additional "layering" one might have available "for sale" to a tenant who could be made a co-beneficiary in the owner's land trust.

Bear in mind that while the selling of these "layers" increases the owner's income, each layer, when "bought" by the tenant, decreases his/her overall housing expense proportionately over time, thereby creating not only reduced after-tax housing costs, but a profitable investment as well.

Note too that any one, or two or three of these so-called *layers* can be "sold" separately, while keeping others, once the tenant is made a beneficiary in the owner's land trust.

For Example:

1. If only the *income tax write-off* is given, the tenant takes a 10% beneficiary interest in the land trust (the minimum allowed by the IRS) and thereby is entitled to 100% of all tax deductions for mortgage interest and property tax paid. This tenant then agrees to relinquish his/her interest at termination for fair consideration. Such *consideration* might be a full or partial refund of any posted contingency fund; payment of moving expenses; payment of first or first and last months rent or mortgage payment on the tenant's next home, etc.).

2. If it is only *Appreciation* that is at issue, the forms needed are only the land trust, an assignment of beneficiary interest and a beneficiary agreement stipulating the amount or percentage of profit to be shared upon termination the trust and disposition of the property.

3. If all (100%) of the property is to be conveyed (a true seller carry-back), then the acquiring party (the tenant in this case) is given a 90% beneficiary interest in the trust, and the 10% settlor (former owner) agrees to forfeit its beneficiary interest when the resident beneficiary refinances the property and returns the nonresident beneficiary contribution (equity at start).

If you truly love something turn it loose. If it belongs to you, it'll come back. But do be sure that when it does, the temporary replacement isn't just stepping out of the shower.

Bill Gatten

A Fortune in Free Real Estate

.

ELEVEN
DOCUMENTATION

The Four Basic Steps to an Equity Holding Trust™ Transfer...

1. Create the Land Trust

2. Create the Beneficiary Agreement

3. Assign or receive a Partial Beneficiary Interest

4. Execute a Lease Agreement (Triple-Net) between the trust and the Resident Beneficiary

WARNING!

Documents shown here, though essentially those used by NARS at the time of this writing, are offered as exhibits only. As presented, these documents may not be suitable in all jurisdictions or could be outdated. Some states may have regulations that may require modifications, additions or appendices which are not included here. In this regard, be aware that neither NARS, its legal counsel, employees, representatives, assigns nor the authors of this book recommend, or accept responsibility for, the use of these forms As-Is.

The reader is advised to seek independent legal counsel relative to the documentation to be used in land trust transfers. Each state has specific rules and regulation that could render one state's documentation unsuitable in other jurisdictions. Examples on the following pages are for illustration purposes only and are not recommended for use.

STEP ONE

THE LAND TRUST AGREEMENT

The land trust form displayed in the following section is essentially the same as that which is the underpinning of the proprietary NARS Equity Holding Trust™ System. Note that when the land trust is created (prior to any assignment of beneficiary interest to a second party), no one other than the original property owner and his/her/their trustee are involved. It is the *subsequent* conveyance of beneficiary interest in the existing trust, and the completion of all of the pertinent ancillary and integrated documentation that conveys the rights and benefits of ownership to other beneficiaries.

TRUST AGREEMENT

Purpose of Agreement. This Trust Agreement, dated ___/___/___ which date is for reference purposes only, shall be known as the _____ Trust, Number _____

This Agreement certifies that appurtenant rights and personal property now used in the general operation of the Real Estate, located in County, State of _____, legally described as:

APN NO. _____ Located at (the "Trust Property") :

1. **When the Trustee has taken title to the Trust Property**, or title to any other property conveyed to it as Trustee under this Agreement, the Trustee shall hold such property, and the proceeds and profits from it, in trust for the ultimate use and benefit of the Beneficiaries and their successors or assigns. The Trustee shall protect and conserve title to the Trust Property until its sale or other disposition. The Trustee shall not manage or operate the Trust Property nor undertake any other activity not strictly necessary to the fulfillment of the purposes set forth above. The Trustee shall not transact business of any kind with respect to the Trust Property which may cause this Agreement to be deemed to be, or which may create the existence of a corporation (de facto or de jure); or a Massachusetts Trust, or any other type of business trust; or an association in the nature of a corporation; or a partnership or joint venture by or between the Beneficiaries, or by and between the Trustee and the Beneficiaries.

117

2. **Beneficiaries.** The person or persons identified in the attached Schedule "A," are the Beneficiaries of this Trust, and as such shall be entitled to all of the proceeds and profits of the Trust Property.

3. **Interests of Beneficiaries as Personal Property.** The interests of any Beneficiary shall consist solely of: a power of direction to the Trustee regarding the Trust Property; the right to receive or direct the disposition of the proceeds from the rentals and from the mortgages, sales, or other disposition of the Trust Property; the right to purchase, lease, manage, and control the Trust Property; and the obligation for expenses and disbursement relative to the property. The right to the proceeds and profits of the property shall be deemed to be personal property. In case of the death of any Beneficiary during the existence of this Trust, the Beneficiary's right and interest shall, except as specifically provided to the contrary in this Agreement, pass to the Beneficiary's executor or administrator. No Beneficiary has now, nor shall subsequently at any time have, any right, title, or interest in or to any proportion of the Real Estate as such, either legal or equitable, nor in any other trust property. A Beneficiary has only an interest in the proceeds and profits, it being the intention of this instrument to vest the full legal and equitable title to the Trust Property in the Trustee. No Beneficiary shall have the right to require partition of any Trust property.

4. **Death of Beneficiary.** The death of any individual Beneficiary, or the merger,

reorganization, or dissolution of any other corporate, partnership, or other form of Beneficiary shall not terminate the Trust nor in any manner affect the powers of the Trustee.

5. **Notice of Assignment of Beneficial Interests.**

a. No assignments of interests by a Beneficiary shall be binding on the Trustee until the original or duplicate copy of the assignment, in such form as the Trustee may approve, is delivered to the Trustee and the Trustee's acceptance is indicated on the assignment. Any assignment not delivered to the Trustee shall be void as to all subsequent assignees or purchasers without notice. The Trustee shall also maintain and revise Schedule "A" of this Trust to reflect any changes in ownership.

b. No assignment of any interest that includes the power to direct the Trustee to convey or otherwise deal with the Trust property, as provided for in Paragraph 12 of this Agreement, shall be valid without the written approval of all the Beneficiaries. No person who is vested with such power of direction, but who is not a Beneficiary, shall assign such power without the written consent of all of the Beneficiaries.

c. Should Beneficiaries opt to convey beneficial interest in this trust, Certificates evidencing the interests of the Beneficiaries may be issued by the Trustee in such form as it may approve, in which event the assignment of the interest shall be valid only upon the surrender of the Certificate, and in which event no assignee shall be entitled to recognition as a Beneficiary until such time as the original Certificate is surrendered to the Trustee along with a proper assignment and until a new Certificate has been issued. However, Certificates shall not be used in the event they would subject The Trust, the Trustee, or the Beneficiaries to state or federal securities regulations from which economical and non-restrictive exemptions would not be readily obtainable.

6. **Tax Returns.** The Trustee shall not be obligated to file any income, profit, or other tax reports, schedules, or returns with respect to this Trust notwithstanding the provisions of Section 671 of the Internal Revenue Code of 1954 or any other applicable regulations. The Beneficiaries shall individually report and pay any taxes on the earnings and proceeds of the Trust property or otherwise arising out of their respective interests. The Trustee shall make available, upon request by the Beneficiaries, accounting records of the Trust which pertain to their respective interests, which records the Trustee agrees to maintain. If it should be found necessary to file Form 1041 or other informational returns under Section 6031 of the Internal Revenue Code of 1954, or otherwise, the Trustee shall not be obligated to prepare the returns, although upon request from the Beneficiaries the Trustee shall, if necessary, sign the informational returns.

7. **Reimbursement and Indemnification of Trustee.** In the event that the Trustee shall make any advance of money on account of this Trust or shall be made a party to any litigation on account of holding title to Real Estate in this Trust or in connection with this Trust, or in case the Trustee,

either personally or as Trustee, shall be
compelled to pay any sum of money on account
of this Trust or any property included in this
Trust, whether on account of breach of contract,
injury to personal property, fines, failure to file
tax returns, or penalties under any law or
otherwise, the Beneficiaries, in accordance with
their respective interests will, on demand, pay to
the Trustee all such disbursements, advances, or
payments made by the Trustee, together with the
Trustee's expenses, including reasonable
attorneys' fees, with interest at the rate of ten
percent (10%) per year, commencing upon the
date of Trustee's disbursement of such funds,
The Beneficiaries will indemnify and hold the
Trustee harmless of and from any and all
payments made or liabilities inured by it for any
reason whatsoever as a result of this Agreement,
including, but not limited to, liability arising from
the management of the trust property pursuant
to a direction by the Beneficiaries. The Trustee
shall be under no duty to convey or otherwise
deal with the Trust property until all of such
disbursements, payments, advances, and expenses
made or incurred by the Trustee have been fully
paid, together with interest. The Trustee shall
not be required to advance or pay out any money
on account of this Trust or to commence or
defend any legal proceedings involving this Trust
or any property or interest held in trust unless
the Trustee shall be furnished with sufficient
funds or be satisfactorily indemnified.

8. **Reliance by Third Parties on Authority of
    Trustee.** No Third Party dealing with the
    Trustee in regard to the Trust Property in any

manner, nor any party to whom the Trust Property or any interest in the Trust Property is conveyed, contracted to be sold, leased, or mortgaged by the Trustee, shall be obliged to see to the proper handling, application, or disbursement of any moneys paid, or to inquire into the necessity or expediency of, or authority for, any act of the Trustee or as to the provisions of this Trust Agreement.

9. **Prohibition Against Recordation.** This Agreement need not be recorded in the recorder's office of the county in which the Trust property is situated, or elsewhere. However, in the event that any such recording shall occur, the recording shall not be considered as notice of the rights of any person derogatory to the title or powers of the Trustee.

10. **Resignation and Replacement of Trustee.**

a. Notwithstanding anything herein contained to the contrary, in the event that the Trustee shall die or become incapacitated, or shall undergo a dissolution, or if the Trustee shall become unwilling or unable to act for any reason, the following, in order of their listing (provided they shall be willing and able to act), shall be appointed as the successor Trustee with the same powers and duties of the predecessor Trustee:

1st Choice: _____

2nd Choice: _____

b. In the event that neither of the above choices is available to serve as the successor Trustee, or in the event that no choices have been designated, the Beneficiaries may appoint a successor Trustee.

A Beneficiary may be named as a successor Trustee. In the event that a successor Trustee is appointed, a copy of this Trust Agreement, together with a Statement of Appointment of the new Trustee and the Acceptance of the Successor Trustee, shall be recorded in the county or counties where the Trust Property is located. The recording shall act to vest title in the successor Trustee with the same powers and duties of the predecessor Trustee, and all other provisions of this Trust shall remain in full force and effect.

c. The Trustee may resign at any time by sending at least a thirty (30) day notice of its intention to do so by certified mail to each of the Beneficiaries at his or her address last known to the Trustee. In the event of the Trustee's resignation, a successor or successors may be appointed by the Beneficiaries, by an instrument in writing which includes the endorsement of the successor Trustee, delivered to the resigning Trustee. The resigning Trustee shall then convey the Trust Property to the successor(s).

d. In the event no successor Trustee is appointed within sixty (60) days from the date of the resignation, the resigning Trustee may convey the Trust Property to the Beneficiaries in accordance with their respective interests and this Trust shall terminate at that time. Alternatively, the Trustee may, at its sole discretion, apply for appropriate relief in any court of competent jurisdiction.

e. Notwithstanding the resignation or replacement of the Trustee, the Trustee (and the

Trustee's estate, if applicable), shall continue to have a lien on the Trust Property for any unpaid costs and expenses, including reasonable attorneys' fees, and for reasonable compensation as may be otherwise provided for in this Agreement until such matters are resolved.

f. Every successor Trustee appointed shall become fully vested with all the estate, properties, rights, titles, powers, trusts, duties, and obligations of its, or their, predecessor-in-trust.

11. **Powers and Duties of Trustee.** So long as the Trustee is the sole owner of record of the Real Estate and any other property held by it under this Trust Agreement, it is understood and agreed by the parties to this Agreement and by any persons who may subsequently obtain an interest in this Agreement, that the Trustee will deal with the property only when authorized to do so in writing by all the Beneficiaries. Also, notwithstanding any change in the Beneficiary or Beneficiaries, it will, on the written direction of the Beneficiaries, or their successors-in-interest, make and execute contracts or deeds for the purchase of or the sale of, execute mortgages, leases, or options on, or otherwise deal with, the Trust Property and with the disposition of the proceeds from any rentals, mortgages, insurance, sales, or other disposition of the Trust Property upon such terms and conditions as may be directed. Nevertheless, neither the Trustee nor any agent employed by the Trustee shall be required, without its consent, to enter into any persona obligation or liability in dealing with the Trust Property or to make itself liable for any damages, costs, expenses, fines, unless it has agreed to do so and has been

appropriately compensated for any acts or services afforded on behalf of the Trust, the Trust Property or the Trust Beneficiaries. To the extent of any moneys due to the Trustee, it shall have a lien on the Trust Property or the proceeds of the Trust Property. The power of direction may be given to a person, corporation, or other form of legal entity upon the written designation of a majority in interest of the persons then entitled to direct the Trustee as to the disposition of the Trust Property, regardless of whether the recipient of the power of direction shall be a Beneficiary. Otherwise, the Trustee shall be required to inquire into the propriety or purpose of any direction.

12.   **Rights and Duties of Beneficiaries.** The Beneficiaries shall have and retain (except as otherwise herein expressly provided) the management of Trust property, and control of the purchasing, renting, handling, maintenance, encumbering, selling, or making of any other disposition of the Trust Property. Expenses shall be allocated according to each Beneficiary's respective interest in the Trust, unless otherwise so agreed. The Trustee shall not be called upon to do anything with respect to the management or control of the Trust Property, the payment of taxes or assessments, insurance, litigation, or otherwise, except on written direction of the Beneficiaries as provided in this Agreement, and after the payment to it of all moneys necessary to carry out the instructions.

13.   **Termination of Trust.** If the Trust Property or any part of the Trust Property remains in the Trust twenty (20) years after the date this Trust was

executed, the Trustee shall give written notice to the Beneficiaries of the proposed termination of the Trust. The notice shall be sent not later than thirty (30) days after the twentieth anniversary date. In the event that an agreement extending the term of this Trust has not been agreed to by all parties within sixty (60) days from the date of the notification, the Trustee shall either convey the Trust Property to the Beneficiaries in accordance with their respective interests; or, upon written direction of all the Beneficiaries or their successors-in-interest, sell the Trust Property at public sale on reasonable notice and divide the proceeds of the sale among all the Beneficiaries in accordance with their respective interests.

14.   **Insurance.** The Beneficiaries agree at all times to carry public liability insurance and such other insurance as the Trustee shall deem necessary or appropriate in the circumstances, insuring the Trust Property, not its contents, and insuring the Trustee in amounts and form acceptable to the Trustee. In the event of the failure of Beneficiaries to furnish the required insurance, the Trustee, in its discretion, after reasonable notice, may procure insurance, without any requirement for comparative cost analysis, and the Beneficiaries do hereby jointly and severally agree that they will pay on demand to the Trustee the amount of the premium on the insurance plus interest of ten percent (10%) per-annum on the amount expended by Trustee for such insurance.

15.   **Compensation of Trustee.** The Trustee shall receive reasonable compensation for its services with respect to this Trust and shall be entitled to

reimbursement of its expenses reasonably incurred. The specific amount, form, and manner of compensation shall be reflected in the attached Schedule "B," which Schedule may be modified from time to time by the approval of all the Beneficiaries or their successors-in-interest, and by the approval of the Trustee. The Trustee shall have no obligation to advance any sums on behalf of the Trust but may do so in its sole discretion. The Trustee shall have a lien on the Trust Property for its fees, expenses, and advances. The Beneficiaries and any persons accepting an assignment of the interest of any Beneficiary agree to pay the fees and to reimburse the Trustee for its expenses and advances on demand. Payment is to be made pro rata based upon each Beneficiary's respective interest unless otherwise agreed among the Beneficiaries. However, as to the Trustee, the payments shall be a joint ad several obligation of the beneficiaries. If the amounts due to Trustee as provided in this paragraph and as provided in paragraph 7 are not paid within sixty (60) days after demand, then the Trustee is authorized and directed by the Beneficiary, for the benefit of the Beneficiaries, to sell the trust property at public or private sale and to transfer and convey sufficient funds to pay for the fees, expenses, and advances, including any additional charges and Trustee compensation which may have arisen or shall arise as a result of the sale. Following the sale, the Trustee shall pay the sale proceeds to the Beneficiaries in proportion to their respective beneficiary interests, following satisfaction of moneys owed to the Trustee. Notwithstanding any other provision of this Agreement, the Trustee shall be under no obligation to make any deed, mortgage, lease, or conveyance of the Trust Property or to enter into any contractual obligation with respect to the Trust Property until its fees are paid and its expenses reimbursed, or until such fee and expenses are secured to its satisfaction.

16. **Binding Effect on Successors.** The terms and conditions of this Agreement shall inure to the benefit of and be binding on any Successor Trustee and on all assigns and successors in interest of the   Beneficiaries

17. **Governing Law.** This Agreement shall be construed and regulated and its validity and effect shall be determined by the laws and regulations of the State of California as such laws may from time to time exist.

18. **Valid Notice Requirements.** Any notice in writing required or permitted to be given to the Beneficiaries by the Trustee or by another Beneficiary will be deemed to have been sufficiently given if actually received or personally delivered, or if mailed by certified mail with return receipt requested, in an envelope addressed to such person at the address shown opposite that person's name in Schedule "A" of this Agreement or at such other address as such person may specify by written notice to the Trustee. Any notice in writing, required or permitted to be given to the Trustee, will be sufficiently given if delivered to the Trustee at its principal office or at such other address as the Trustee may specify.

19. **Restrictions on Transfers of Beneficial Interests.** Prior to the termination of the trust agreement, any Holder of a beneficial interest

desiring to sell or dispose of the beneficial interest, or any portion thereof, at any time, must first offer to sell the interest to the other Beneficiaries, if any, according to their respective proportionate beneficial interests. The beneficial interest for sale must be offered at the same price as the highest written good faith offer by a Third Party to purchase the interest, at a price mutually agreed upon by the parties, or at a price determined by an M.A.I. appraisal of the corpus of the Trust. An option for the purchase of the interest shall be given to the remaining Beneficiaries for a period of thirty (30) days. If the option is accepted, the purchasing Beneficiaries shall have the right to purchase the interest for a lump-sum payment in cash within ten (10) days after the exercise of the option, or payment may be made upon terms agreeable to both the purchasing and selling Beneficiaries. If the option is not accepted within the thirty-day period, the beneficial interest may then be offered to any Third Party. However, the other Beneficiaries hereunder are given an option for an additional period of ten (10) days to meet the price and terms at which it is proposed to sell the interest to the Third Party if the terms have changed. If the Beneficiaries meet the price, the sale shall be made to them, for a lump-sum payment in cash or upon other mutually agreeable terms, within ten (10) days after the exercise of the subsequent option. This shall not interfere with the right of any Beneficiary to transfer a beneficial interest by will or gift. The beneficial interest, however, shall be subject to this provision in the hands of all future Beneficiaries, including heirs, executors, administrators, personal representatives, donees, successors, and assigns. The terms of this provision respecting the transferability of beneficial interest may be modified by agreement of all of the Beneficiaries, in writing.

20. **Amendment, Modification, or Termination of Agreement.** This Trust Agreement contains the entire understanding between the parties and may be amended, revoked, or terminated only by a written agreement signed by the Trustee and all of the Beneficiaries or their designees, except that termination may result from the operation of this Agreement.

21. **Non-liability of Trustee.** All obligations incurred by the Trustee shall be the obligations of the Trust only, and shall not under any circumstances be the individual obligations of the entity acting as Trustee unless the Trustee specifically consents in writing to such liability. No Beneficiary shall have any authority to contract for, on behalf of, or in the name of the Trustee, or to bind the Trustee personally, unless the Trustee's consent is first obtained in writing.

22. **Beneficiary Cannot Bind any Other Beneficiary.** Except as specifically set forth elsewhere in this Agreement, or provided for in law relative to community property, no Beneficiary shall have the authority to contract for or in the name of any other Beneficiary or to bind any other Beneficiary personally.

23. **Addition of Other Property to Trust.** Additional property may at any time be conveyed to the Trustee under this Trust, and such property and the proceeds shall be held, dealt

with, and disposed of under the terms of this Agreement and in the same manner as the property specifically described. The terms and conditions of the deed or other manner of transaction by which such property is conveyed to the Trustee shall constitute and be construed as a part of this Agreement. The Trustee shall maintain the attached Schedule "C," which shall identify all property held by this Trust.

24. **Perpetuities Saving Clause.** Notwithstanding any other provisions of this Agreement, if any portion of the Trust estate is in any contingency capable of being held in trust for a longer period than is permitted by law, or if in any such contingency the vesting of any interest may occur after the expiration of such permissive period, then upon the happening of such contingency all of the Trust estate shall not be held further in trust, and the Trust estate assets shall be divided, transferred, conveyed, and delivered to the Beneficiary or Beneficiaries in accordance with their respective beneficial interests hereunder. The Trust shall then terminate by operation of law.

Trustee _____   Beneficiary_____

By: _____   Beneficiary_____

Dated: _____   Dated _____

STEP TWO

THE ASSIGNMENT OF BENEFICIARY INTEREST

The *Assignment of Beneficiary Interest,* used when conveying interest in a simple trust, is analogous to a bill-of-sale in that it validates and confirms any acquisition and disposition relative to such interest.

It is this document that conveys a specific percentage of personal property beneficiary interest in the Land Trust, and in the trust property's income and profit potential. The consideration for such assignment is generally the new co-beneficiary's posting of some or all of the trust's Contingency Fund.

The Assignment is the basis for the legitimate transfer of all or part of the personal property beneficiary interest in the trust from one party to another. The agreement is between, and executed only by, the relinquishing beneficiary (assignor) and the assignee beneficiary.

ASSIGNMENT OF BENEFICIAL INTEREST

Recitals:

A. Transferor is the owner of beneficial interest in the _____ Trust, Number _____, dated __/__/__, ("the Trust") with _____ as Trustee thereof.

B. The Trustee currently holds legal and equitable title to the real estate together with all of its appurtenances, improvements and equipment, which property is located at _____, in the city of _____ and more particularly described as follows:

C. Whereas _____ desires to acquire the beneficiary interest of the party known as _____ and to reside in the above described real property held by the Trust: within this document the assignee, _____, shall be referred to as the "New Beneficiary" and assignor, _____, shall be referred to as the "Former Beneficiary."

NOW THEREFORE, the parties hereto have agreed as follows:

1. **Assignments.** Former Beneficiary hereby conveys to New Beneficiary all of the rights and interest to the beneficial interest held by Former Beneficiary in the _____ Trust, along with a proportionate share of the Power of Direction associated with that beneficial interest.

2. **Consideration.** Former Beneficiary is transferring the beneficiary interest in the Trust to New Beneficiary in consideration of payment by New

Beneficiary of $_____ and an agreement by New Beneficiary to faithfully perform all obligations and responsibilities of Former Beneficiary pursuant to Section 4 below.

3. **Closing.** The parties' effective execution of this document shall act to convey the specified beneficial interest in the _____ Trust. Such execution shall be effective upon the receipt by Former Beneficiary of the amount shown in Para. 2, and payment in full of all required trustee fees. The parties shall also execute such other documents as may be necessary relative to completion of the subject transfer of beneficial interest.

4. **Assignment and Assumption.** New Beneficiary hereby assumes all of the rights, benefits, duties and obligation of Former Beneficiary under the _____ Trust and the related Beneficiary Agreement, Occupancy Agreement and all other existing related Documents.

5. **Entire Agreement.** This contract comprises the entire agreement of the parties regarding the assignment of this beneficial interest in the _____ Trust and no other representations or agreements relative to this assignment have been made or relied upon. This contract shall be binding upon the parties and any successor or assign.

The parties acknowledge that this document has been prepared by _____ _____ and overseen by Attorney, _____, at the request of the beneficiaries of the trust, and that neither preparer or the referenced attorney, are in any manner representing any party to the subject transaction. The parties are directed to obtain their own legal, real estate and financial advice in this matter.

Consent to Transfer

By: _____Transferor

By: _____Transferor

Date: __/__/__

Transfer completed (received)

By: _____Transferee

By: _____Transferee

Date: __/__/__

STEP THREE

THE BENEFICIARY AGREEMENT

The Beneficiary Agreement can be thought of as analogous to a partnership agreement between (among) co-beneficiaries. It is used following the conveyance of an interest (all or part) in the land trust that is the underpinning of the NEHTRUST™

This document sets out and defines the respective obligations, benefits and restrictions of all of the parties (beneficiaries) to the NEHTRUST™. It directs how the distribution of funds relative to the trust property are to be handled at the termination of the land trust and any related lease agreement wherein a co-beneficiary would be a tenant.

The Beneficiary Agreement and its addendum set out the respective percentages of beneficiary interest held by parties, and the order and priority of distribution of all proceeds resulting from the sale or other dispositions of the property at termination.

BENEFICIARY AGREEMENT

This Agreement is dated __/__/__ for reference purposes only, and is entered into by and between the undersigned, all of which are or will become Beneficiaries of a NARS Equity Holding Trust arrangement relative to a land trust agreement dated __/__/__, and known as the _____ Trust, No. _____ (the "Trust"), under which _____ _____ shall be the Trustee.

1. **In General.** Under the provisions of the Trust, the Beneficiaries collectively have certain rights, powers, duties and obligations reserved to them including, but not limited to, the following:

    a. Power of direction to authorize the Trustee to deal with title to Trust property;

    b. Right to receive or direct the disposition of proceeds from rentals, mortgages, sales, or other dispositions;

    c. Right and duty of management of Trust property, and control of the purchasing, renting, handling, encumbering, selling, prosecuting evictions, and collection of rents and proceeds; and

    d. Obligation for the expenses and disbursements relative to the property.

2. **Collection and Disposition.** The parties agree that the rights, powers, duties, and obligations reserved to them relative to the subject transaction shall be administered as follows:

a. All customary payment collection functions shall be delegated to _____ _____ who may in turn contract with outside vendors for these services. These functions include, but are not limited to, the right to receive or direct the disposition of any contingency fund provided by the parties for curing any default or delinquency, including payment for trustee services in connection therewith, the right to receive or direct the disposition of proceeds from rentals, mortgages, sales, or other dispositions; prosecuting evictions, and control of the purchasing, renting, handling, encumbering, selling, and collection of rents and proceeds; and the obligation for the expenses and disbursements relative to the property.

b. Any bill-paying/collection service selected by beneficiaries shall not be a property management company and shall not charge a fee for its services. Neither shall it forward any moneys received with respect to the Trust Property unless it has been given sufficient funds by the beneficiaries with which to make all payments then due to creditors of record: including payment of any fees due to the trustee for the subject land trust, even if the failure to forward such sums would create a default in underlying primary financial obligations relating to the Trust Property.

3. **Disposition at Trust's Termination.**

a. Subject to a first right to purchase set forth below, the Trust property shall be sold at the trust's termination. The process of such disposition shall begin with delivery of a Purchase

Offer (the "Offer") by Certified Mail no later than four (4) months (120 days) prior to termination of this Agreement (e.g., 4 months prior to __/ __/__).

b. _____'s first right to purchase shall begin with the date of this Agreement and shall terminate upon the sale or other disposition of the Property. Before the property is sold, it shall first be made available for sale to _____ on terms and at a price equal to that which would be proposed for a sale of the Property to a third party. _____ shall have ten (10) days from receipt of the Purchase Offer from __/__/__ (the "Offer Period") in which to accept or reject the Offer. _____'s right to reject the Offer shall expire at 5:00 PM. on the last day of the Offer Period. The Offer shall contain the proposed sale price (which shall include _____'s right to offset the sale price by the value of _____'s share of profits and any co-beneficiary contributions which are mutually agreed by parties to have been paid by, and be refundable to _____ _____). The Purchase Offer shall also include the specific financing or refinancing terms; the required earnest money deposit; the time and place for the close of escrow; and any other material terms and conditions upon which the proposed sale is to be based and consummated. _____ shall not be obligated in any manner to assist in the purchase financing or refinancing arrangements relative to the Purchase Offer and _____ _____'s

139

acquisition of the property. If _____ _____ gives timely notice of acceptance of the Purchase Offer, then _____ _____ shall be obligated to purchase the Property at the price and on the terms and conditions of the Offer. If _____ does not, within the allotted ten (10) day Offer Period, give timely notice of rejection with a reasonable counteroffer, based upon the Fair Market Value of the property as determined by an M.A.I. ("Member American Institute of Real Estate Appraisers") appraisal, then the Offer shall be deemed to have been accepted in full as made.

4.   **Co-Ownership; Division of Profits.** The parties acknowledge that they have no direct ownership of the Trust Property but only personal property interests in the Trust. The parties expressly disclaim any relationship among each other as that of partners or in partnership, and the parties further agree that they are merely co-beneficiaries and co-owners in relationship to each among the other. The parties shall share in the earnings and in the expenses, gains, and proceeds of the Trust Property as set forth in the Priority of Distributions Section referred to in Exhibit A to this Agreement.

5.   **Funds.** A non-interest bearing checking account shall be maintained by the Trustee for the subject Trust, which account shall require the signature of an authorized representative of _____ for withdrawal. All cash receipts from the Trust Property shall be promptly deposited in the account, and all

operating expenses relating to the Trust or Trust Property shall be paid from that account.

6. **Books of Account.** Should the parties wish to independently appoint an accountant or bookkeeper for keeping records of the subject property and its financial affairs, full and accurate books of account shall be maintained by such accountants or bookkeepers as may from time to time be designated by the parties.

7. **Expenses and Contributions.**

a. Interest in the subject Trust Property is being acquired solely for investment purposes. No party shall have any authority to obligate the other parties for any expense or liability in connection with the property or to contract or deal with the property on behalf of the other parties in any manner, except as may be specifically provided in paragraph 2 of this Agreement. Each party shall be liable only for his proportionate share of the mutually agreed-upon acquisition value at the inception of this agreement and for other expenses relating to the Trust or the Trust Property.

b. A Beneficiary may be entitled to possession of the Trust Property only pursuant to an occupancy agreement substantially in the form accompanying this Agreement. A Resident Beneficiary's obligation to pay rent under the Occupancy Agreement shall be deemed an obligation to contribute funds necessary to accomplish the Trust's purposes.

ANY BENEFICIARY WHO MAY RESIDE IN THE TRUST PROPERTY

ACKNOWLEDGES THAT ITS RIGHT OF POSSESSION OF THE TRUST PROPERTY ARISES SOLELY BY VIRTUE OF A SEPARATE OCCUPANCY AGREEMENT AND IS SUBJECT TO EVICTION PROCEEDINGS UNDER APPLICABLE LAWS AND UNLAWFUL DETAINER STATUTES IN THE EVENT OF DEFAULT UNDER THE TERMS OF SUCH AGREEMENT, OR DEFAULT UNDER THE TERMS OF THIS BENEFICIARY AGREEMENT. THE DEFAULTING PARTY ALSO AGREES THAT IT SHALL REMAIN SEVERALLY FULLY RESPONSIBLE FOR ALL COSTS OF EVICTION AND ANY RELATED LEGAL EXPENSES AND COURT COSTS.

c. Failure by any party to contribute, on a timely basis, his share of funds necessary to accomplish any of the purposes for which the property is held or to pay any of the expenses in connection with the property, shall, at the option of the majority in interest of the other parties create a debt from the delinquent party to the other parties in the amount of the liability, plus interest at the rate of ten percent (10%) per annum until paid. Any uncollected balance may be collected by lawsuit or by charging against any income or proceeds which may otherwise be due to the delinquent party. A delinquent balance extending for longer than thirty (30) days shall be considered, at the option of a majority in interest of the other parties, as an offer by the delinquent party to sell his beneficial interest under paragraph 19 of the Trust for an amount equal to the delinquent party's proportionate interest in the Property at the time of default less the amounts described below. The delinquent party's interest shall be valued as of the date of default by obtaining, within thirty (30) days of default, an appraisal of the Property providing for immediate sale. Notwithstanding the provisions of paragraph 19 of the Trust, payment for the beneficial interest of the delinquent party shall be in the form of an unsecured promissory note, bearing simple interest at the rate of ten percent (10%) per annum, with the principal and interest due and payable on the sale or refinance of the Trust Property.

PARTIES ACKNOWLEDGE THAT IT WOULD BE IMPRACTICAL TO DETERMINE ACTUAL COSTS AND DAMAGES RELATIVE TO A DEFAULT OR DELINQUENCY. THE PARTIES REASONABLE ESTIMATE OF SUCH COSTS WOULD BE TWO THOUSAND DOLLARS ($2,000.00), AND THAT SUCH AMOUNT, TOGETHER WITH ANY SUM CERTAIN PREVIOUSLY OWING FROM THE DELINQUENT PARTY TO THE TRUST, SHALL BE DEDUCTED FROM ANY AMOUNT PAYABLE TO THE DELINQUENT PARTY FOR THEIR INTEREST IN THE TRUST PURSUANT TO THIS PARAGRAPH AND RELATIVE VERBIAGE IN THE SUBJECT LAND TRUST.

8. **Property Improvements.** Homeowners Association bylaws, regulations and CC&R's notwithstanding, the Resident Beneficiary may not make material alterations or improvements to the Trust Property without the prior written consent of the Trustee and the Non-Resident Beneficiaries, which shall not be unreasonably withheld. The beneficiaries shall have the right to approve or disapprove contractors, plans and specifications. If such improvement or alteration increases the fair market value of the Property, as determined by an independent appraiser selected by the Beneficiaries and paid for by the Resident Beneficiary, then the Resident Beneficiary shall be credited with a contribution to the Trust in the amount of such increase in value as of the date of completion.

9. **Transfer and Sale of Beneficial Interest.** Each party shall have the right to sell, give, or bequeath all or any part of his beneficial interest to any other party, subject to the provisions of paragraph 19 of the related Trust Agreement for Trust No _____ and payment of required transfer fees. No such divestiture can take place without the express knowledge and agreement by the majority of all other beneficiaries, and such agreement shall not be unreasonably withheld.

10. **Amendments.** Any party may petition the Trustee and the other Beneficiaries to add to or modify any provision of the Trust, the Occupancy Agreement, or this Agreement. Any such additions or modifications shall require the written approval of all parties, which may be granted or withheld in the sole discretion of each party.

11. **Binding Agreement.** The terms and conditions of this Agreement shall inure to the benefit of and shall be binding upon all parties, being all of the beneficial interest in the subject Equity Holding Trust™ arrangement and their assigns and successors-in-interest.

All parties whose signatures appear below acknowledge having read the above in its entirely, and that they understand it clearly and agree to its terms and condition without request for alteration or amendment.

_____ Date _____
Beneficiary

_____ Date _____
Beneficiary

_____ Date _____
Beneficiary

_____ Date _____
Beneficiary

EXHIBIT "A"

TO BENEFICIARY AGREEMENT

Beneficiary Interest, Ownership, Shared Appreciation, Respective Contributions:

TRUST AGREEMENT TERMINATES ON: __/__/__

NON-RESIDENT BENEFICIARY: _____
[I.D. No. _____], whose address is _____

_____, shall hold a ___ percent (_____%) beneficiary interest in the Trust No. _____.

NON-RESIDENT BENEFICIARY: _____
[I.D. No. _____], whose address is _____
_____, shall hold a ___ percent (_____%) beneficiary interest in the Trust No. _____.

RESIDENT BENEFICIARY: _____
[I.D. No. _____], whose address is _____
_____, shall hold a ___ percent (_____%) beneficiary interest in the Trust No. _____.

PRIORITY OF DISTRIBUTION OF PROCEEDS AT TERMINATION OF AGREEMENT:

Upon termination of trust, proceeds from sale or disposition of the trust property shall be distributed as follows:

First, all encumbrances against the property shall be paid in full.

Second, all relevant costs of disposition of the property (e.g., RE commissions, closing costs, advertising, etc.) upon termination shall be paid.

Third, any Nonresident Beneficiary Contribution* shall be paid to Nonresident Beneficiary.

Fourth, any Resident Beneficiary Contribution* shall be paid.

Fifth, all remaining proceeds from sale or other disposition of property shall be distributed to beneficiaries with respect to each of their percentages of ownership of beneficiary interest in the subject NARS Equity Holding Trust™.

NONRESIDENT BENEFICIARY CONTRIBUTION:
$_____

Non-Resident Beneficiary's initial contribution shall normally include the nonrecurring costs in Escrow ($_____) as of this date, plus the difference between the accepted value of subject property (i.e., its "Mutually Agreed Value") at inception [$_____] and the existing loans secured by it [$_____], which amount shall not include: RE commissions paid at the inception of this transaction, mandatory recurring costs (e.g., regular monthly payment amounts, taxes due, late fees, etc.), or other charges or penalties incurred by Non-Resident Beneficiary.

RESIDENT BENEFICIARY CONTRIBUTION:
$_____

Resident Beneficiary's initial contribution normally is to consist of: all nonrecurring costs contributed in the form of: closing costs $_____, including any contribution to existing equity ("equity buy-down"), and/or any portion of RE commissions paid by Resident Beneficiary. The amount shown here may also be increased at the transaction's termination to include costs of mutually accepted and agreed-upon expenditures for repairs or capital improvements to the property (a certified *Letter of Agreement* stipulating the exact amount of such mutually accepted and agreed-upon expenditures and work to be done is mandatory).

Beneficiaries initials: _____   _____

STEP FOUR

THE OCCUPANCY/POSSESSORY AGREEMENT

The Occupancy Agreement that is related to, but separate from, the Illinois land trust at the center of the Equity Holding Trust™ process must always be a "Triple Net Lease." A *triple-net lease* stipulates that the responsibilities for mortgage payments, the property's maintenance, and insurance are fully those of the Lessee (AKA: *net-net-net* lease).

It is imperative that one clearly understands that in order to avoid the potential for characterization of the entire transaction as a *disguised security agreement, equitable mortgage, partnership, corporation* or *homeowner's association,* the lease must not contain or be related to a purchase option, contain any reference to ultimate acquisition of the property or carry a term of more than three years (a *day-to-day holdover* may, however, be stipulated following the expiration of the lease agreement). There can be no "bargain buy-out," or any interest consideration or payment of interest between tenant and landlord.

> The lease payment should always be an aggregate amount covering all the components of the monthly obligation: loan principal, mortgage interest, hazard insurance, property tax and other assessments.

OCCUPANCY AGREEMENT

This Occupancy Agreement is dated __/__/__ for reference purposes only and is between _____ _____ as Trustee of the _____ _____ Trust, No. _____, ("Landlord"), and _____ ("Tenant").

1. The Landlord agrees to lease to Tenant the premises commonly known as _____, California ("the Premises").

2. Subject to Paragraph #4 below, Tenant hereby contracts to pay the sum of **$**_____ per month as it may from time to time be adjusted, which rental payment and obligation may include, but may not be limited to, the following:

    a. A Trustee Fee in the amount of $_____.

    b. The principal and interest, as they may from time to time be adjusted, on all loans secured by the Premises.

    c. Premiums for all necessary insurance on premises, as set forth herein, as they may from time-to-time be adjusted.

    d. Property taxes on premises, as set forth herein, as they may from time-to-time be adjusted.

e. Association fees (if/when applicable), as they may from time-to-time be adjusted

4. In the absence of a full Security Deposit, rents and any other payments due shall be made in advance to the Landlord's agent,

    _____

    _____, on or before the 15th day of the month preceding the date of the month in which such payments are ordinarily due to the creditors of the Trust which holds the subject leased property. Should a reserve in the minimum amount of one full monthly obligation have been placed on deposit with, and maintained by, Landlord agent, then the payment may be considered due and payable on or before the first day of the month in which such payments are due to the creditors. Rent is payable by check, by mail, at the following address:

5. If at any time any increases or decreases occur in element of the rental obligations set forth above, the total monthly rental shall increase or decrease by the same amount, and any the contingency fund be adjusted accordingly.

6. Tenant agrees to pay to the landlord a late charge of two percent (2%) of the total outstanding balance of rent owed, if the rent is not received within 10 days of its due date. This late charge does not establish a grace period. Landlord may make written demand for payment if rent is not paid on its due date. Landlord and Tenant agree that the charge is presumed to be the damages sustained because of Tenant's late payment of rent, and that it is impracticable or extremely difficult to fix actual damages.

7. Tenant agrees to pay a service charge of $20.00 if Tenant's bank returns a rent check for insufficient funds (NSF). If the bank returns Tenant's rent checks more than once, Landlord may serve written notice that all future rent be paid in cash or by certified check or money order.

8. The term of this Occupancy Agreement will commence on __/__/__, and Tenant agrees to indemnify Landlord for any liability arising before termination of this Occupancy Agreement for personal injuries or property damage caused by the negligent, willful, or intentional conduct of Tenant, and Tenant's guests or invites.

9. Tenant will deposit with Landlord's agent the sum of $_____ as a security deposit. The total amounts of which shall become part of the Contingency Fund relative to the trust in which title to the leased property is held, which Contingency Fund requirement may be adjusted in the event that the monthly payment obligation is adjusted. The Landlord's agent will hold the above deposits to insure the faithful performance by Tenant of Tenant's obligations under this Occupancy Agreement, including payment of rent and, after surrender of the Premises, cleaning of the Premises, repair of the Premises exclusive of ordinary wear and tear, and to remedy any default in Tenant's obligation under the Occupancy Agreement to restore, replace, or return personal property or appurtenances, exclusive of ordinary wear and tear. Within two weeks after Tenant has vacated the Premises, Landlord's agent will furnish Tenant with an itemized written statement of the basis for, and amount of, the security

received and its expenditure, and will return any remaining portion of the security deposit to Tenant.

13. If Landlord's agent applies all or any portion of Tenant's security deposit during the term of this Occupancy Agreement to cure a default or make necessary repairs to the Premises, Landlord's agent may demand that Tenant replenish the full amount so applied. Tenant's failure to replenish such amount within five days after written demand will constitute a material breach of this Occupancy Agreement. The written demand for replenishment will include an itemized statement describing the disposition of the security.

14. Tenant shall pay all real property taxes and assessments, whether general or specific, which are, or may later be, levied against the Premises.

15. Tenant agrees that the Premises, fixtures, appliances, and furnishings are in satisfactory condition.

16. Tenant shall, at Tenant's expense maintain full insurance coverage on the leased property, including replacement value coverage, insuring the Landlord in an amount not less than $_____. Tenant shall deliver to the Landlord certificates evidencing the existence of such insurance. No policy may be canceled without the prior written consent of the Landlord. Tenants contents insurance shall be acquired at tenant's option.

17. Tenant may not assign Tenant's interest under this Occupancy Agreement, or sublet any portion of the Premises.

18. Any attempt by Tenant to assign or sublet all or any portion of Tenant's interest under this Occupancy Agreement will be null and void and ineffective to transfer such interest to any person.

19. The Premises are rented to Tenant for residential purposes only, and may not be used by Tenant for any other purpose.

20. Tenant is responsible for payment of all utilities and service charges related to occupancy of the Premises.

21. Tenant agrees to perform the following obligations:

a. To keep the Premises as clean and sanitary;

b. To dispose of all rubbish, garbage, and other waste in a clean and sanitary manner;

c. To use and operate properly all electrical, gas, and plumbing fixtures and pipes, and to keep them as clean and sanitary as their condition permits;

d. To refrain from willfully or wantonly destroying, defacing, damaging, impairing, or removing any part of the Premises or the facilities, equipment, or appurtenances, or permitting any person on the Premises to commit such acts;

e. To occupy the Premises as Tenant's abode, using designated portions of the Premises for living, sleeping, cooking, and dining purposes; and

f. To comply with any Covenants, Conditions and Restrictions regarding the Premises.

22.   Tenant may not use the Premises for any unlawful purpose, violate any law or ordinance, or commit waste or nuisance on the Premises.

23.   Before making any repairs for defective conditions on the Premises, Tenant must first notify Landlord of the need for such repairs: See: Para. 3.

24.   Tenant may not make material alterations to the Premises without first obtaining Landlord's written consent, which may not be unreasonably withheld. On completion, any such repairs or alterations become part of the Premises.

25.   Repairs and maintenance expenditures are fully the responsibility of Tenant: though no amount of such expenditure shall be refundable or credited to Tenant, unless such work is done at the written direction of Landlord (_____, the Trustee for the _____ Trust), following tenant's notification of the necessity of such work and request for credit for expenses relative thereto. Such notification and request for credit must be by certified mail, delivered to Trustee in care of the Collection Company at the address shown herein, and must be accompanied by pertinent bona fide bids, quotes or estimates.

26.   On not less than 24 hours' advance notice, Tenant must make the Premises available, at a time acceptable to Tenant during normal business hours for entry by an agent of the Landlord for the purpose of periodic inspections. In case of emergency, upon Tenant's abandonment or surrender of the Premises, or with a court order, Landlord's agent may enter the Premises at any time without securing Tenant's prior permission.

27. The parties consider each term, covenant, and provision of this Occupancy Agreement to be material, reasonable and legally binding.

28. For any breach of any covenant or condition of this Occupancy Agreement Landlord may, at it's option, serve a three-day notice (1) specifying the nature of the breach and (2) demanding that Tenant cure the breach if it can be cured. The notice may further declare that, if Tenant fails to cure a curable breach within the three-day period or if the breach is not curable, the tenancy is terminated and Tenant forfeits all rights under this Occupancy Agreement. The question of whether breach of a covenant or condition is curable will be determined by the prevailing law in the State of California as of the time of service of a three-day notice specifying that Tenant's alleged breach is a non-curable breach. Landlord may also take such actions as are specifically provided for in the Trust Instrument and Beneficiary Agreement to which Tenant and Landlord are parties.

29. If Tenant willfully and maliciously remains in possession of the Premises after expiration of the tenancy, Landlord may recover three times the amount of any damages and rent due, as punitive damages.

30. After Tenant vacates the Premises, either by expiration of the term or on termination of the tenancy, Landlord must give the notices required by law concerning disposition of any personal property of Tenant that remains on the Premises. Tenant is responsible for all reasonable costs of storing such personal property. The property will

be released to Tenant or its rightful owner only after Tenant or the rightful owner pays to Landlord the reasonable costs of storage within the time required by law.

31. If Landlord is unable to deliver possession of the Premises to Tenant at the commencement of the term specified in this Occupancy Agreement, Landlord will not be liable for any damage caused thereby, nor will this Occupancy Agreement be void or *voidable*. Landlord will take reasonable steps to obtain possession of the Premises from previous tenants or occupants. Tenant will not be liable for any rent, however, until the date that possession is actually delivered. Tenant may cancel this Occupancy Agreement if Landlord fails to deliver possession of the Premises within 60 days after commencement of the specified term.

32. In any legal action brought by either party to enforce the terms of this Occupancy Agreement, the prevailing party is entitled to all cost incurred concerning such an action, including reasonable attorneys' fees.

33. Waiver by either party of a breach of any covenant of this Occupancy Agreement will not be construed to be a continuing waiver of any subsequent breach. Landlord's receipt of rent with knowledge of Tenant's violation of a covenant does not waive Landlord's right to enforce any covenant of this Occupancy Agreement. No waiver by either party of a provision of this Occupancy Agreement will be considered to have been made unless expressed in writing and signed by all parties.

34.   Time is of the essence of each provision of this
        Occupancy Agreement.

35.   This Occupancy Agreement, together with the
        Trust and the Beneficiary's Agreement, between
        the parties, and their related documents contain
        all the agreements of the parties and cannot be
        amended or modified except by written
        agreement.

36.   For the purpose of service of process and service
        of notices and demands, Tenant's address is:

        _____

        _____

37.   Notices, demands, and service of process for
        Landlord may be served by _____,
        which is the entity authorized to collect payments
        and make disbursements relative to this
        agreement, and whose usual address is:

        _____

        _____

Landlord: Tenant:

_____   _____

Date: _____   Date: _____

END NOTES

[1] The type of trust utilized and referred to throughout this book is an inter vivos (*living), revocable, beneficiary-directed title-holding (Illinois-type) land trust*

[2] The property's bare legal and equitable title is conveyed for a specified period of time to a neutral third-party trustee, who acts on behalf of, and is directed by mutual agreement of, the beneficiaries.

[3] The *Garn-St. Germain Law* (FDIRA 1982) protects borrowers from foreclosure due to a lender's claim of a *"due-on-sale"* violation, when a property's title is conveyed to an express, revocable, living trust in the name of the borrower, and which does not convey occupancy rights (though a subsequent and separate lease agreement can, of course, convey such rights). Therefore: creation of the land trust doesn't invoke the due-on-sale clause; leasing the property doesn't trigger the due-on-sale clause (assuming a term of less than 3 years, and that there is no option to purchase); and... a subsequent designation of a co-beneficiary is unrecorded and involves assignment of *personal* property only – not the loan's real property security.

[4] Anytime there is equity in the property at start, it is the seller who determines how much "down," if any, will be required from the buyer. Any equity *not* so *purchased* by the buyer is "carried" by the seller as a *Nonresident Beneficiary Contribution*, to be collected when the property sells, or is refinanced, at the termination of the mutually agreed-upon term of the trust.

[5] Unless the seller were to be insolvent at the time, a "short-sale" or foreclosure would likely result in the lender's issuance of an IRS form 1099. The amount reflected would be taxable to the seller. The difference between what the property is sold for, and what is[was] owed on the loan/s against it is seen by the IRS as income to the "forgiven" party. The 1099 might also include, as well, any unpaid payments, fees, late charges, and possibly even all the lender's costs of disposing of the property.

[6] Credit qualifications of the NARS NEHTrust™ buyer are established and evaluated solely by the seller, and are most often based upon similar criteria as might be employed in screening a renter or lease tenant.

[7] Title 12 of the U.S. Code (para. 1701j-3) permits the formation of a revocable inter vivos trust by a borrower, in which trust the property can be held for the benefit of the borrower for asset protection purposes. This congressional LAW also specifically allows for the 'letting (renting or leasing)' of the property for up to three years, so long as there is no purchase option related to the lease, and so long as the lease is not a part of the trust document itself.

[8] Def: A "Short-Sale" is a discounted mortgage payoff, wherein a portion of a borrower's debt is forgiven by the lender. The debt relief granted is taxable in the year it is received, and the relieved borrower will likely receive a derogatory credit report entry indicating that the mortgage obligation was not met as agreed. In addition, a bank's agreement to grant a short-sale is often very time consuming and tenuous at best (and is wholly dependent upon there being a willing and ready buyer).

[9] When NARS arranges for the trusteeship with Partners with America Corporation or Equity Holding Corporatiton, the preferred corporate trustees for the NEHTrust™, ancillary collection and disbursement is provided free of charge.

[10] A division of ownership between beneficiaries can be established at the beginning, so that proceeds upon final disposition can be distributed between them. Distribution is in proportion to each beneficiary's respective contribution to the trust (e.g., amount of equity carried, amount of closing costs paid, cost of mutually agreed-upon capital improvements during the term of the agreement, etc.).

[11] NARS' collection affiliates can handle such matters for the parties when so requested.

[12] Non residential real property may be exchanged for other investment real estate instead of creating a taxable sale. Revenue Ruling #92-105 "... provides that beneficial interest in a

land trust, even though characterized as *personalty*, may be exchanged for *realty*, under the rules of an IRC §1031 Like-Kind Tax-Deferred Exchange."

[13] An IRS *Notice of Fiduciary Responsibility* Form No. 56 is filed by the trustee, at the beginning of the trust, on behalf of the beneficiaries.

[14] See *R&TC* – e.g., §§ 62(a) & 64: see generally R&TC §§58-63.

[15] The history of the land trust, which has become the base for the NARS NEHTrust™ System, has its beginnings in feudal England, under the reign of King Henry VIII, more than 550 years ago.

[16] Black's Law Dictionary, 6th Ed., West, 1990.

[17] A Grantor's Trust, in which one party serves all elemental functions, will likely be characterized by the IRS as a "dry" or "failed" trust, lacking purpose or objective, and be taxed as a corporation. A second [co-] beneficiary in such a trust would likely be denied tax benefits relative to real estate ownership, because the "equitable title" and tax benefits in a Grantor's Trust remains with its grantor and not the trustee or beneficiaries (IRC §§ 671-677); Black's Law, 6th Ed., 1990, p. 700.

[18] The *Illinois Land Trust*, after which all other states' land trusts are modeled, was developed by Chicago Title, Chicago, Illinois, circa 1920. Its earliest use was primarily for the benefit of certain influential individuals of the day who owned large amounts of Real Estate, but who preferred that their names not show up in the public record (in its earlier years, it was off-handedly referred to as the "Mafia Trust").

[19] DEF: Inter vivos - *Created during the lifetime of the settlor (i.e., grantor).*

[20] DEF: *Legal Title* is ownership evidenced by a deed or mortgage; *Equitable Title* is one's given rights in and to the ownership of the property, and the right to be treated fairly under the law (under the "rules of Equity") relative to the facts of

ownership, and to participate in the property's possession, occupancy, appreciation, etc.).

[21] IRS guidelines require that any beneficiary of a business entity who intends to claim income tax benefits needs to be at least a ten percent stockholder. This means that if all beneficiaries are seeking income tax benefits in a land trust, there could be no more than ten of them. Otherwise there is no particular limit to the number of beneficiaries that a land trust can accommodate. Although, should there be more than a few, the entire transaction could be deemed a security, thereby triggering the rules and restrictions of a stock offer of "security" in the eyes of state or federal securities regulators.

[22] IRS §702, §676, §163, §167(h) & IRS Reg. No. 25.2702-5(c)(1)-(7)

[22] Since the trustee holds both *legal* and *equitable* title, its beneficiaries can hold personal property interest only, which means that such ownership form may be treated as *real property* for income tax purposes, and *personal property* in other legal contexts (e.g., as it relates to partition-ability). Because both the "legal" and "equitable" interest in the real property corpus of the trust are held by a third-party trustee, the personal property ownership of multiple beneficiaries is *non-partition-able* for purposes of satisfying judgment creditor liens. For that reason, the existence of a "remainder agent" or co-beneficiary can prevent a forced-sale of the property to satisfy judgment liens, tax liens, or bankruptcy action. This arrangement even thwarts actions by an ex-spouse whose interest may have been conveyed earlier (by deed or quit claim).

[23] Because both the *legal title* and *equitable title* in a land trust property are held by a third-party trustee, the personal property ownership of multiple beneficiaries becomes, for all practical purposes, *non-severable* ("non-partitionable') and impervious to charging orders stemming from the satisfaction of judgment creditor claims. For these reasons the existence of a co-beneficiary (*successor beneficiary* or *remainder agent*) can thwart the forced-sale of the property to satisfy a judgment lien,

tax lien or legitimate bankruptcy action. Such co-beneficiary protection may even obstruct a claim by an ex-spouse who would have deeded the property to the trust in a state of sound mind.

[24] The IRS characterizes the transfer into or out of a land trust as a "nonevent" in terms of transfer, conveyance, or reconveyance of real estate.

[25] Re: *Garn-St. Germain* (FDIRA 1982). See endnote #3.

[26] i.e., Consideration, Mutuality of Agreement and Obligation as well as Competent Parties and Subject Matter.

[27] See IRC §163(h)(4)(D) Re: "Qualified Residence" - Special Provisions for Estates and Trusts" (i.e., estates and trusts that hold equitable title to, and interest in, real estate).

[28] Ibid.

[29] Commercial, agricultural or industrial property can be held in land trusts in which the beneficiaries are assigned various benefits responsibilities, profit incentives, powers of direction and percentages of future profits.

[30] DEF: *Hypothecation* is the pledging of a property as security for performance on a financing arrangement in which the ownership of the property doesn't change unless there is a breach of the promise to pay or perform a required duty (re. a "performance deed," e.g., say, re. a secured note or equipment lease).

[31] It should be noted that any predetermined buy-out or other advance agreement involving one party's purchasing the interest of the other, would likely cause IRS characterization of the transaction as a "disguised security agreement." The contract provides simply that the resident beneficiary shall be given the first right to acquire the property for an amount equivalent to its then fair-market-value, less the amount of any financial equity, if any, held by the purchasing party.

[32] Though final documents do not contain such verbiage, should the resident beneficiary purchase the property at the trust's termination, the parties can, if they so choose, mutually agree to forgo formal appraisal. The value would then be determined by

any means by which they mutually agree. The IRS will, however, likely deem any predetermined stated intention to purchase, or pre-stated buy-out figure, as a disguised mortgage loan, and possibly deny certain tax benefits.

[33] This provision allows the first beneficiary (the settlor) the choice of either - 1) reducing the amount due him/her, or 2) having the property returned to him/her.

[34] Even if shown as an *"Offer In Compromise - Paid As Agreed,"* a new lender is likely to balk at issuing credit to someone who has a record of "walking away" from a debt obligation due to circumstances which were clearly not the fault of the previous lender.

[35] It is arguable that if one were to record a *Deed in Lieu*, granting title to the lender, that the lender couldn't report the loan as having been [being] in default, if no payments were missed.

[36] See Garn-St. Germain Law (FDIRA). Leases which grant leasehold interest for more than 3 years, or which contain options to purchase constitute valid cause for a lender's demand for the payoff of its loan.

[37] An *AITD* or *AIM* (All-Inclusive Trust Deed or All-Inclusive Mortgage, often called a "Wrap," is a loan which "wraps around" previously existing loans secured by the property and incorporates them within it. As an example, anyone intending a 100% financing arrangement on, say, a $100,000 property with a 1st mortgage of $50,000 and a 2nd mortgage of $25,000, could make a loan of $100,000 to the buyer, with monthly payments sufficient to cover the obligations on the other two loans with some left over every month for the seller.

[38] From the date of the "Contract of Sale," a party entering a real estate exchange, in order to avoid capital gains tax, has only 180 days to locate the replacement property and close the transaction. If the Land Contract is not a Contract "OF" Sale, and is merely a Contract "FOR" Sale [at a future time], then it is unlikely that tax benefits will accrue to the *vendee*. In most so-called Land Contracts, the ultimate acquisition

[purchase] of the property takes place considerably more than 180 days from commencement of the contract.

[39] i.e., this is relative to the "non-partitionability" of personal property to satisfy a creditor judgment.

[40] Re. The Garn-St. Germain Act – The *Federal Depository Institutions Regulations Act, FDIRA 1982* [supra]. This congressionally enacted federal law was framed to protect mortgagors (borrowers) from the erratic, often malicious, foreclosure practices of state, federal and private lenders prior to 1982. Likewise a secondary purpose of the FDIRA was to allow lenders clear-cut parameters relative to their right to terminate a mortgage loan if their security interest would become compromised or imperiled by the actions of a borrower. It was determined by the FDIRA that under most circumstances a lender could call its loan due and payable if the property's title were transferred in any manner without its express knowledge and consent.

Today, one's transfer of a property's ownership to an inter-vivos trust in which one remains a beneficiary and which trust does not involve a transfer of occupancy rights is excluded under the law (GSG) as a cause for a lender's acceleration of a mortgage loan. (See Footnote # 3.)

[41] Note that, although Contingency Fund contributions of more than one monthly payment are optional, NARS does encourage the posting of *two* or more such incremental amounts when possible, and/or when at all feasible.

[42] Beneficiaries of a land trust may not utilize a *paid* property manager (should they do so, the IRS could classify the arrangement as an association, double-taxing it as a corporation and potentially denying active tax write-off for the resident beneficiary).

[43] IRS guidelines re. Land Trusts require that the trust's beneficiaries must manage the trust property themselves... without the assistance of a paid property management company. Employing a professional management company (i.e., licensed, bonded, fee-based, etc.) would undoubtedly force the characterization of the NEHTrust™ as a general partnership, a corporation, or as an association or cooperative (taxed as a

corporation).

[44] Example: A $170,000.00 property with a 5-year old, 30 year loan at 7.5%, with a balance owing of $185,000, commands a monthly payment of, say, $1,370 for 25 remaining years. In calculating an *Effective Interest Rate (EIR)*, one would consider the PV (present value) to be $170,000.00; the PMT (payment) to be $1,370.00; the N (term) to be 300 months (i.e., 25 yrs x 12 mos). By solving for Interest, this calculation will reveal an Effective Interest Rate of 8.51%.

Note that if an over-encumbered property would fail to appreciate or yield a profit, the over-encumbrance, during the term of the agreement, a payoff needn't be considered if the investor or resident beneficiary decide to just "walk away" at the transaction's termination.

[45] E.g., see 103 Ill.App 3d. 174. 430 N.E.2d 708 (2d Dist) 1981 Wachta v. 1st Fed. S&L, and Damen v. Heritage Bank respectively; Williams v. 1st Fed. S&L, Arlington Va., #80-308A, 6/17/80, et al.; La Sala v. Am. S&L, 5 Cal. 3d 864, 489 P.2d 1113, Cal.App. 91. Cal. Rptr. 238; 97 Cal. Rptr. 849 (LA No. 29851 Sup. Ct. of CA); Coast Bank v. Mindenhout, 61 Cal. 2d 311, 317 (38 Cal. Rptr. 505, 392 P2d 265); Title 12 USCA 1701j-3.

[46] Re. *Rule Against Perpetuities*, see Hatfield, *Perpetuities in Land Trusts*, 40 Ill I.Rev. 4, 110 (1945); see *Kenoe on Trusts* §2.67 (IICLE, 1989); Hart v. Seymore, 147 Ill.598, 1614, 35, N.E., 246 (1893).

Services

Carefully note here that North American Realty Services, Inc. (NARS), and the co-authors of this book are actively in the business of acquiring residential real estate (1-4 units) via the methods described in this book. Should the reader have or know of such an opportunity, wherein a current seller (for a full-price offer, without commissions or closing costs) might benefit from our program (by retaining the current mortgage financing in place, and leaving some or part of any existing equity in tact for from 2 to 10 years), please contact us regarding participation and/or referral fee information.

Contact:

Bill Gatten or
Jan Caldwell, Esq.
North American Realty Services, Inc.
6520 Platt Avenue #548
West Hills, CA. 91307
Phone 1 800 207 4273
E-mail: home@landtrust.net

Products

Products

Various other NARS products and services for investors, Realtors and other industry professionals include:

- Full NEHTrust™ and PACTrust™ Documentation service, assistance and legal review
- Trustee and collection service setup
- Workshops and Seminars throughout the U.S.
- Personal one-on-one coaching training and mentoring in all aspects of creative real estate acquisition
- Extended training courses on tape and CD, including all books, courses, documentation, training aids, by-state legal indices, sales aids, recordings of actual sales and transaction dialogue, etc.
- The NARS Bi-monthly Investor Bulletin and newsletter (to sign up go to www.landtrust.net and enter your name and e-mail address - it's free)
- The NARS National Professional Network - providing all of the above, plus properties for those with cash, and cash for those with properties, along with unlimited ground-partnering program in all states (i.e., one member puts up any needed cash while another, the *ground partner,* shows and manages the property)
- Weekly 1 to 1.5 hour continuing telecoaching training session for all students and NARS Network members
- *Making it BIG and Keeping it...This Time,* with searchable CD. The down-to-Earth creative real estate investing primer (for newbies and old salts alike) featuring the NARS Equity Holding Trust™. This fully searchable 500 page book delves into all matters of creative real estate acquisition and financing. It includes a state-by-state index of legal codes and cites, How-To's in all aspect of Creative Financing (irreverent, humorous and VERY educational)

Notes

For additional copies of:

A Fortune in Free Real Estate

_____ # Books @ $16.95 each $_____

Shipping/handling $_____
$2.95 per book, by regular mail:

Sales tax, if California order: $_____
$1.66 per book

Total $_____

☐ Check, payable to NARS, Inc.

☐ AMEX   ☐ Visa   ☐ Mastercard

Card Number: _____

Expiration: _____

Name: _____

Address: _____

_____

North American Realty Services, Inc.
6520 Platt Avenue, #548
West Hills, CA 91307
(800) 207-4273
www.landtrust.net   e-mail: home@landtrust.net

A Fortune in Free Real Estate